Estate Planning the Middle Income Client

Second edition

Estate Planning for the Middle Income Client

Second edition

By
John Thurston LLB, Solicitor, TEP

Tottel publishing

Tottel Publishing Ltd, Maxwelton House, 41–43 Boltro Road, Haywards Heath, West Sussex, RH16 1BJ

A CIP Catalogue record for this book is available from the British Library.

ISBN: 978 1 84592 487 4

Typeset by Laserwords Private Ltd, Chennai, India

Printed and bound in Great Britain by Antony Rowe, Chippenham, Wilts

Preface

This book is specifically aimed at anyone who is advising the average middle-income clients, the clients whose houses in most parts of the country can be worth way in excess of the nil rate band for inheritance tax purposes, but who do not have a huge amount of capital beyond the house. These clients sometimes become very concerned about the amount of inheritance tax which will be payable on the estate of a surviving spouse because of the increase in the value of houses, and the failure of the nil rate band for inheritance tax purposes to keep pace with this increase.

The book is divided into two parts. The first part is an explanation of the basic principles of taxation applicable to wills and settlements. The second part contains ideas for advising the middle-income client about how to save inheritance tax. However, it must be remembered that in advising clients, saving inheritance tax is only one factor to be taken into account, and that there may be other considerations which mean that saving inheritance tax is irrelevant, or no more than a minor element in the advice given to clients.

I believe that the schemes discussed in the second part of the book are viable, but it should always be borne in mind that whilst a scheme may be viable at the moment, it may not work in years to come because of a challenge by HMRC, or a change in the law. I have tried to include a comprehensive coverage, but inevitably there may be some points that have been omitted.

I have used the masculine for the sake of simplicity, but obviously it includes the feminine.

This is the second edition of this book. As with the first edition, I welcome any comments, suggestions or feedback; please send these to the publishers, who will forward them to me.

John Thurston
July 2007

Contents

Contents

Contents

Contents

Table of cases

Table of statutes

Table of statutes

Chapter 1

Introduction—Basic Principles

1.1   This book is designed to help professionals advise the middle income client—the typical client who owns the home jointly with his or her spouse or a cohabitee, and may or may not have additional capital. As readers will be well aware, the value of houses, particularly in London and the South East and also many other regions in the United Kingdom, will frequently exceed the nil rate band for inheritance tax purposes. Clients are often well aware of the inheritance tax implications of this increase in value of houses having read newspaper articles on the matter, and frequently seek advice on what can be done to mitigate this liability.

It is important that clients should be aware that the rules or HMRC practice may change. One such change was announced in the Budget Statement on 10 December 2003. The Finance Act 2004 contained provisions introducing a charge to income tax on preowned assets still used by the donor or donors. This charge had retrospective effect, and came into effect in April 2005. The effect of the charge is to charge income tax on the notional market rent of any house given away but still used by the donor or donors, where there has been no reservation of benefit. It also catches gifts of chattels still used by the donor or donors, where the reservation of benefit rules do not apply, and in such a situation there is a charge to income tax on a percentage of the capital value of the asset.

Another change to the taxation of trusts was the completely unexpected change to the taxation of trusts contained in the Finance Act 2006. This Act substantially changed the inheritance tax treatment of trusts, and is considered in subsequent chapters.

Apart from the desire to save inheritance tax (IHT), another motive for giving the home to children is to avoid the proceeds of sale of the home being used to pay care home fees. Whilst there is no doubt that care home fees can quickly exhaust the value of the home, it should be remembered that it is only a relatively small percentage of the population who are forced to go into a home, and that the length of stay is usually quite short. In addition, clients who are concerned about care home fees should consider whether they wish to surrender the right to choose where they wish to live because, if the gift is successful, they may have little choice over which home they go to. Furthermore, there may be enough income to pay care home fees without resort to capital.

It should always be borne in mind that tax planning is only one factor to be taken into account when advising a client. There are many other personal factors which may be more important than any tax planning consideration. For example, second or third marriages or cohabitations are very common. Frequently the parties wish to ensure that adequate provision is made for the survivor, but ultimately each will wish to ensure that their children inherit their property. This is clearly a more important factor than any tax planning considerations.

It is also desirable that any tax planning scheme should be as simple as possible. If the objective of the client can be obtained by making use of the lifetime exemptions from inheritance tax, then use should be made of those exemptions.

There may be pressure from the middle income client to take action *inter vivos* to save IHT, but in many cases it is arguable that they should not do so. They would be best advised to do nothing because they may need all the capital they have to provide for themselves.

The author does not pretend that the book contains a complete list of all the options open to the middle income client, but it is hoped that all the main options have been considered.

It is believed that most of the ideas in the book are viable, but there is always an element of risk that they will not work, and clients should be warned of this possibility. Most, if not all, of the pitfalls have been highlighted.

It goes without saying that the professional adviser must not be involved in any scheme which could constitute a criminal offence as far as the HMRC are concerned.

This book is divided into two parts. The first part is an introduction to tax, and will be of interest to those who are new to this field, or need a refresher. The second part is concerned with tax planning.

In order to prevent clumsiness, the masculine has been used throughout this book; obviously, this includes the feminine.

PART I

Chapter 2

Inheritance Tax—Introduction

In common with all other taxes, inheritance tax (IHT) is the creation of statute. It was originally called Capital Transfer Tax, and caught both lifetime and death transfers. The main charging Act is now the Inheritance Tax Act 1984, which has been amended by subsequent Finance Acts.

WHEN DO YOU PAY IHT?

2.1   IHT is payable on five occasions since 22 March 2006:

- death;
- absolute gifts if the donor dies within seven years or transfers to trusts for disabled persons—otherwise known as potentially exempt transfers (PETs);
- lifetime chargeable transfers—transfers into any settlement apart from a trust for a disabled person;
- ten-yearly or principal charges—all trusts apart from immediate post death interests, trusts for disabled persons and trusts for bereaved minors;
- exit or proportionate charges—all trusts apart from immediate post death interests, trusts for disabled persons and trusts for bereaved minors.

Prior to 22 March 2006 it was only payable on death, absolute gifts if the donor died within seven years, and lifetime transfers into discretionary trusts. In addition, if there was a discretionary trust whether in a will or a lifetime settlement, then there was a possibility of a charge every 10-years, the principal charge, and also exit or proportionate charges whenever the trustees handed out any capital or a beneficiary became absolutely entitled under the terms of the trust.

Death is the most frequent occasion which triggers IHT, although in the past it has only been payable in respect of a comparatively small number of estates. This may change due to the increase in the value of houses.

If a client has made a large gift or a series of gifts to, say, a child or grandchild, then although IHT is not due when the gifts are first made, it may have to be paid if the donor dies within seven years of the gift. These gifts are known as potentially exempt transfers or PETs.

Since 22 March 2006, if a client creates or transfers property to any trust apart from a trust for a disabled person during his lifetime, then IHT will have to be paid if the transfer is large enough. Trusts for disabled persons are discussed in more detail at **5.3**. Prior to 22 March 2006, these treatments would only have applied to discretionary trusts. A discretionary trust is one where there is a class of beneficiaries, commonly spouse, children and grandchildren, who do not have any rights to anything. It is totally at the discretion of the trustees as to who benefits, and to what extent. In addition, if the client dies within seven years of the creation of the settlement, the IHT must be recalculated.

A charge to inheritance tax, the principal charge, is imposed every 10-years on the capital in all trusts apart from trusts for disabled persons, immediate post death interests and trusts for bereaved minors, and there is also an exit charge or proportionate charge whenever any capital leaves such a trust. Prior to 22 March 2006, these charges only applied to discretionary trusts.

RATES (2007/2008)

2.2   There are two rates—the nil rate band (NRB) for transfers up to £300,000 (for the year ending 5 April 2008), and 40% for transfers above that figure.

The NRB is one of the reasons why IHT has been paid on few estates on death. A large number of estates have been within the NRB, and so no IHT was payable on them. However, the recent surge in house prices has meant that more estates exceed the NRB.

The NRB is usually increased each year in line with inflation, quite often at more than the general rate of inflation but less than the rate of inflation of house prices.

The rate for a lifetime transfer is one-half of the rate which applies on death.

The rate for a 10-yearly charge is currently 30% of the lifetime rate, 6%.

VALUE TRANSFERRED

2.3   On death the deceased is deemed to have disposed of all his property at market value.

If it is a lifetime transfer or gift, IHT is paid on the reduction in value of the transferor's estate. Normally this is the same as the value of the property given away, but not always. If the donor makes a lifetime transfer of shares in a quoted public company, the value of the shares given away will be the same as the reduction in the value of the donor's estate. However, if the donor owns a set of antique dining chairs, a set may be worth more than individual chairs. So if the donor gives one chair to a child, then the value chargeable will not be the value of one chair; it will be the reduction in value of the estate—the difference in value between a set of, say, six chairs, and a set minus one chair.

Another example is, if the donor has a controlling shareholding in a company. A controlling shareholding is worth far more than a minority holding, and so if a controlling shareholder makes a gift, and reduces his shareholding to a minority holding, the reduction in value of his estate is not the value of the shares the subject of the gift, but the difference in value between a majority shareholding and a minority shareholding. Frequently such a gift will not have any IHT consequences as the shares will qualify for 100 per cent business property relief.

CUMULATION

2.4 IHT is a cumulative tax. This means that in determining the rate of tax applicable to a transfer—0% or 20% or 40%—previous transfers must be taken into account. The cut-off point is usually seven years.

So in determining the rate of tax which applies to a transfer either during the lifetime of the donor or settlor or on death, it is necessary to go back seven years to see what other gifts have been made by the donor or the deceased.

Example

D gives £500,000 to his only child.

Six years later he dies.

In determining the rate of tax which applies to his death estate, it would be necessary to go back seven years to see if the NRB has been exhausted by lifetime gifts. It clearly has been—assuming that the NRB is £300,000—and therefore the whole death estate will be subject to IHT at 40 per cent.

EXEMPTIONS AND RELIEFS

2.5 There are various exemptions and reliefs from IHT which substantially reduces the burden, and frequently means that no IHT is payable.

Some exemptions and reliefs apply only to lifetime transactions, whereas others apply to both lifetime transactions and death.

Exemptions and reliefs applying to lifetime gifts

2.6   These are considered in more detail in **Chapter 19**.

(*a*)   *Annual exemption:* £3,000 per annum; if it is not used, it can be carried forward for one year, but not to subsequent years.

£3,000 is not a very large amount on its own, but if a client can give away £3,000 for 20, 30 or 40 years, it can amount to a quite a large saving in IHT. However, there are not many clients who can afford to do this and provide adequately for themselves, a surviving spouse or cohabitee. The annual exemption has not been increased for many years.

(*b*)   *Normal expenditure out of income:* As long as a client can maintain a normal standard of living, then he can give away the remainder of his income. So if the client is earning £1.5 million, and can maintain his standard of living on £1 million, then he can give away the remaining £0.5 million without incurring any liability to IHT.

The exemption also applies to persons on lower incomes. If the client is earning £30,000 per year, and can maintain his standard of living on £20,000, he can give the remaining £10,000 away without incurring any liability to IHT.

(*c*)   *Marriage or civil partnership exemption:* Gifts on the occasion of a marriage or civil partnership are exempt up to certain limits depending on the relationship. If it is the parent making the gift, then the exempt amount is £5,000. Again, the exempt amounts have remained the same for many years.

(*d*)   *Gifts for the maintenance of the family:* If a client has a child at university, and gives money to that child, strictly each gift is a PET for IHT purposes. This exemption means that it will not be chargeable to IHT.

'Family' is widely defined—obviously it includes children, but it can also include parents. So if, for example, a client helps his widowed mother, this will not give rise to any charge for IHT.

(*e*)   *Small gifts:* Small gifts of up to £250 per person per year are exempt. The main reason for this exemption is that otherwise these gifts would be PETs. It would be very unpopular and unworkable if Christmas presents etc were classified as PETs. Again the exempt amount has not been increased for many years.

Exemptions and reliefs applying to lifetime gifts/death

2.7

(*a*) *Gifts to charities and political parties*

(*b*) *Agricultural property relief (APR) and business property relief (BPR)*
APR and BPR operate by reducing the value of the property transferred by 50% or 100% for IHT purposes. If the reduction is 100%, it
means that property is exempt from IHT as far as BPR is concerned.

(*c*) *Spouse exemption* There is no IHT on transfers between spouses,
provided the donee spouse is domiciled in the United Kingdom. The
exemption applies both to *inter vivos* gifts and transfers on death. If
the donee spouse is not domiciled in the United Kingdom, then the
exemption is limited to £55,000. If the donor spouse has not used
up his NRB, then that amount can also be given to the surviving
spouse in addition to the £55,000. There is a similar exemption for
civil partners.

SUMMARY

Since 22 March 2006 IHT has been payable:

- on death;
- absolute gifts if the donor dies within seven years or transfers to trusts
  for disabled persons—otherwise known as PETs;
- lifetime chargeable transfers—transfers into any settlement apart from
  a trust for a disabled person;
- ten-yearly or principal charges—all trusts apart from immediate post
  death interests, trusts for disabled persons and trusts for bereaved
  minors;
- exit or proportionate charges—all trusts apart from immediate post
  death interests, trusts for disabled persons and trusts for bereaved
  minors.

In order to determine the rate of tax, it is necessary to take account of
previous transfers.

IHT is payable on the reduction in value of a donor's estate if it is a lifetime
gift.

On death IHT is payable at the market value.

Chapter 3

IHT on Death

NO LIFETIME GIFTS

3.1   If the deceased has not made any lifetime gifts, and no exemptions and reliefs apply, then the whole of the death estate will be taxable at 40 per cent in so far as the nil rate band (NRB) is exceeded.

Example

Assume NRB is £300,000.

A dies leaving an estate of £500,000.

Deduct the NRB of £300,000, which leaves a taxable estate of £200,000.

Inheritance Tax (IHT) at 40 per cent on £200,000 = £80,000.

If the whole estate had passed to the spouse, who is domiciled in the United Kingdom, then no IHT will be payable because of the spouse exemption.

LIFETIME GIFTS COVERED BY A LIFETIME EXEMPTION OR RELIEF

3.2   If the deceased had made lifetime gifts, but these are covered by some exemption, then they are ignored when calculating the rate of IHT applicable to the death estate. For example, if the deceased has made gifts of £3,000 each year, these will not affect the rate of IHT payable on death as each will come within the annual exemption.

Example

Assume NRB is £300,000.

B makes one lifetime gift of £6,000.

Exempt—B can make use of the current year's annual exemption plus the annual exemption from the previous year.

B dies leaving an estate of £600,000.

Deduct the NRB of £300,000 = £300,000.

IHT at 40% on £300,000 = £120,000.

LIFETIME GIFTS WITHIN SEVEN YEARS OF DEATH

3.3   If the deceased had made lifetime gifts within seven years of death which are not covered by any exemption, these must be cumulated in order to determine whether the NRB has been exhausted, and therefore to determine the rate of tax applicable to the death estate. If the NRB has been exhausted, then IHT at 40 per cent is payable on the whole death estate. If not, then whatever is left of the NRB can be offset against the death estate.

Example

Assume NRB is £300,000.

C makes a lifetime gift of £300,000.

He dies five years later leaving an estate of £500,000.

The whole of the death estate is subject to IHT at 40 per cent.

Example

D makes a lifetime gift of £206,000.

He dies three years later leaving an estate of £500,000.

Assuming D has not made any other lifetime gifts, deduct two years annual exemption from £206,000 = £200,000.

Deduct £200,000 from NRB = £100,000.

£100,000 of the NRB is left to offset against the death estate.

IHT at 40 per cent on £500,000 − £100,000 = £160,000.

Another way of calculating the IHT applicable to the death estate is to calculate the IHT applicable to the total of the death estate and the lifetime gifts, and then deduct any IHT applicable to the lifetime gifts (this is the method adopted in the IHT 200).

If this method is adopted in the last example, IHT on the total of the lifetime gifts and the death estate (£700,000) after deducting the NRB is £160,000.

As the lifetime gifts are within the NRB, there is no deduction to be made from the IHT applicable to the death estate.

If the lifetime gift had been £400,000 after deducting any exemptions, IHT on the total of the lifetime gifts and death estate would have been £900,000 − £300,000 = £600,000 at 40% = £240,000, less IHT on the lifetime gift in so far as it exceeds the NRB (£100,000 at 40% = £40,000). So the amount of IHT payable on the death estate would be £240,000 − £40,000 = £200,000.

The same answer would have been reached if the lifetime gifts had been treated as absorbing the NRB, so that the whole of the death estate was taxable at 40%. IHT on £500,000 at 40% is £200,000.

It should be noted that the £40,000 is not necessarily the amount of IHT payable in respect of lifetime gifts. It is necessary to do a separate calculation for each lifetime gift, and IHT payable in respect of the lifetime gift may be reduced by taper relief.

SUMMARY

3.4

- No lifetime gifts, and no exemptions and reliefs—any part of the death estate above the NRB is taxable at 40 per cent.
- Lifetime gifts within the seven years before death must be taken into account.

Chapter 4

IHT on PETs

WHAT IS A PET?

4.1   A PET is an absolute gift, or since 22 March 2006, a transfer to a trust for disabled person; these are considered in more detail at **5.3**. Before 22 March 2006, a transfer to the trustees of a life interest trust, or a transfer to the trustees of an accumulation and maintenance settlement would also have been a PET.

WHAT DOES 'PET' MEAN?

4.2   PET means potentially exempt transfer, and a lifetime gift or transfer is called so because no inheritance tax (IHT) is payable when the gift or transfer is first made. It only becomes payable if the donor dies within seven years of the gift or transfer—the gift or transfer has the potential to become exempt.

ONE PET

4.3   If there is only one PET, then it will be chargeable to IHT if the donor dies within seven years of the gift, except in so far as it comes within one of the lifetime exemptions from IHT. The nil rate band (NRB) is offset against the PET before it is offset against the death estate.

Example

Assume NRB is £300,000.

E makes a PET of £506,000.

He dies within two years.

Assuming E has not made any other lifetime gifts, deduct two years annual exemption from £506,000 = £500,000.

Deduct NRB of £300,000.

IHT at 40 per cent on £200,000 = £80,000.

Example

Assume NRB is £300,000.

F makes a PET of £106,000.

F dies within two years.

Assuming F has not made any other lifetime gifts, deduct two years annual exemption from £106,000 = £100,000.

The PET is not chargeable as it is within the NRB.

However, only £200,000 of NRB is left to offset against the death estate.

SEVERAL PETS

4.4   If the donor has made several lifetime gifts, then all those prior to the PET within seven years of death must be cumulated together in order to determine the rate of tax which applies to that PET. A separate calculation for each PET is required.

Thus it is necessary to look back seven years from the date of death, and add together all the PETs made prior to the one you are dealing with and within seven years of death in order to determine the rate of tax—and whether the NRB has been exhausted.

Example

Assume NRB is £300,000.

Assume that all lifetime reliefs have been used.

G makes a PET of £150,000 within three years of death.

He also makes another PET of £350,000 within one year of death.

No IHT will be payable on the PET of £150,000 as it is within the NRB of £300,000.

It absorbs £150,000 of the NRB, leaving £150,000 unabsorbed.

IHT payable on the PET of £350,000 is £350,000 − £150,000 = £200,000. 40 per cent of £200,000 = £80,000.

Example

Assume NRB is £300,000.

Assume that all lifetime reliefs have been used.

H made the following PETs:

£100,000 in 1998.

£250,000 in 2004.

£300,000 in 2006.

H dies in March 2007.

2004 and 2006 PETs are clearly chargeable.

2004 PET—the 1998 PET can be ignored as it is more than seven years before death. As the 2004 PET is within the NRB, no IHT is payable.

2006 PET—ignore the 1998 PET. The 2004 PET absorbs £250,000 of NRB, leaving £50,000 unabsorbed.

£250,000 of the 2006 PET is taxable at 40% = £100,000.

The NRB is fully exhausted by PETs—all the death estate will be chargeable to IHT at 40%.

TAPER RELIEF

4.5   If the donor dies three or more years after making the gift, then taper relief will reduce the amount of IHT payable.

Death between three to four years—20% reduction.

Death between four to five years—40% reduction.

Death between five to six years—60% reduction.

Death between six to seven years—80% reduction.

It should be stressed that taper relief only reduces the IHT payable. It does not reduce the value transferred for any purposes.

Example

Assume NRB is £300,000.

Assume that all lifetime reliefs have been used.

I makes a PET of £400,000.

I dies three-and-a-half years later.

IHT at 40% on PET after deducting NRB = £100,000 at 40% = £40,000.

Taper relief—as T has survived for three years after making the gift, there is a 20% reduction, so only 80% of the tax is payable. The IHT payable is therefore £32,000.

However, in determining the rate of tax which applies to the death estate, the full value of the gift must be brought into account.

SUMMARY

4.6

- No IHT is payable on PETs when first made.
- IHT is payable if the donor dies within seven years of making the gift.
- The PET must then be cumulated with other gifts made prior to that PET and within seven years of death.
- Taper relief may reduce the amount of IHT payable.

Chapter 5

Overview of the Taxation of Trusts

IMMEDIATE POST DEATH INTERESTS, TRUSTS FOR DISABLED PERSONS AND TRUSTS FOR BEREAVED MINORS

The Finance Act 2006 substantially changed the law about the taxation of trusts as far as inheritance tax is concerned. The Act did not make any major changes to capital gains tax, although the changes to the inheritance tax treatment of trusts have made hold-over relief more widely available. In addition, the Act did not change the rules about the income tax treatment of trusts.

Inheritance tax

5.1   As a result of the Finance Act 2006 all trusts are taxed for inheritance tax (IHT) purposes as if they are trusts without an interest in possession; they are subject to the 'relevant property regime'. This means that IHT will be payable on the lifetime creation if a settlor transfers assets in excess of the nil rate band (NRB) to such a trust. The rate of IHT is one-half of the rate which applies on death—20 per cent. In addition, there will be a charge to IHT every 10 years, and there will also be an exit charge or proportionate charge whenever any capital leaves the trust. At the moment the rate of IHT is low—30% of the lifetime rate, 6%.

There are, in effect, three exemptions from these rules:

1. Trusts created on death for the benefit of one life tenant—'an immediate post death interest'.
2. Trusts created either in the settlor's lifetime or on death for a disabled person as defined in s 89 of the Inheritance Tax Act (IHTA).
3. Trusts created on death by a parent for a minor child.

What all this means is that if someone creates a trust in their lifetime and it is not a trust for a disabled person, then as far as IHT is concerned it will be treated as if it was a trust without an interest in possession or a discretionary trust and subject to the relevant property regime. This means that IHT will be payable on the creation of the trust at 20 per cent on all assets transferred to the trust in excess of the NRB or what is left of the NRB. In addition, there will also be charge to IHT every 10 years on the assets in the trust. There will also be an exit or proportionate charge to IHT whenever the trustees distribute any capital to a beneficiary either exercising powers or because the beneficiary has become absolutely entitled under the terms of the trust. The rate of IHT is not very high—it cannot be more than 6 per cent, but it is still an additional tax.

Trusts in wills will also be taxed as if they were trusts without an interest in possession unless the trust comes within the three exemptions.

These three exemptions are fairly narrowly targeted, and it is necessary to look at each in turn.

Immediate post death interest

5.2   The following conditions must be satisfied for an immediate post death interest:

1.   The settlement must be effected by will or under the law relating to intestacy.

2.   The life tenant must have become beneficially entitled to the interest in possession on the death of the testator or intestate.

3.   Section 71A does not apply to the property in which the interest subsists or the interest is not a disabled person's interest.

4.   Condition 3 has been satisfied at all times since the life tenant became beneficially entitled to the interest in possession.

The first condition requires that the settlement must arise on death. So the settlement must either be created in a will, or it could arise under the intestacy rules.

If someone dies intestate leaving a spouse or civil partner and children and a large enough estate, then the surviving spouse or civil partner will be entitled to a life interest in one-half of the residuary estate. That will be an immediate post death interest.

The second condition requires that the life tenant should become beneficially entitled to the interest on the death of the testator or intestate. This means that the life interest cannot be postponed until some future time; it must come into immediate effect on the death of the testator, not in, 10 years time. However, a survivorship clause of up to 6 months is alright. In addition, if a will creates successive life interests, then the first can be an immediate post death interest, but not subsequent ones. These would be subject to the relevant property regime.

Section 71A is concerned with trusts for bereaved minors. So, if the trust is a trust for a bereaved minor, then it is not an immediate post death interest. In addition, if it is a trust for a disabled person then it is not an immediate post death interest.

Condition 4 requires that condition 3 must have been satisfied since the life tenant became entitled to the interest.

If conditions are satisfied, then the life tenant is deemed to own all the underlying trust assets as far as IHT is concerned. This means that there will not be any ten-yearly or principal charges or proportionate or exit charges, but when the life tenant dies, the assets in the trust will be aggregated with the life tenant's personal estate.

Example

1. T makes a will transferring assets to A for life then to B

Note that the trust must be in a will. It would be alright if the life tenant can only take if they survive for a period not exceeding 6 months. This would still be treated as if the life tenant had an interest in possession. So there will not be any 10-yearly charges or exit charges, but IHT will be payable on all the assets in the trust on the death of the life tenant.

If it is a lifetime creation, then it will be subject to the relevant property regime and will be taxed as if it was a trust without an interest in possession. IHT will be payable on creation if the reduction in value of the settlors' estate is large enough, and there may be 10-yearly or principal charges to IHT, and also exit or proportionate charges.

Trusts for disabled persons

5.3   The second exemption is concerned with trusts for disabled persons as set out in s 89 of the IHTA.

To come within s 89, the beneficiary must be a disabled person as defined in the section. In effect they must be mentally incapable or in receipt of attendance allowance or disability living allowance. So it is possible to have a discretionary trust, and the class of beneficiaries could include the disabled person along with other family members. There must also be a term that, if the trustees decide to hand out any capital, at least one-half must go to the disabled person.

If a settlor creates a trust in his lifetime for a disabled person, and complies with the rules in s 89(4) of the IHTA 1984, then it will not be taxed as if it was a trust without an interest in possession or a discretionary trust; instead it will be taxed as if the disabled person had an interest in possession. This means that there will be no charge to IHT if the settlor creates one of these trusts during his or her lifetime. It will be a potentially exempt transfers (PETs), and as long as the settlor survives for seven years, it will not have any adverse IHT consequences.

If the testator creates a trust for a disabled person in his will, then IHT will be payable on the death of the testator if the testator's estate is large enough, or the NRB has been absorbed by lifetime gifts in the seven years prior to death, in accordance with the normal rules about the taxation of estates on death.

However, there will not be any 10-yearly or exit or proportionate charges, but IHT may be payable on the death of the disabled person as the settled assets will be aggregated with the disabled person's personal assets.

The definition of a trust for a disabled person has also been extended so as to include trusts where the disabled person has a life interest.

This was not necessary under the old law as, if a disabled person had a life interest, then the disabled person would be deemed to own the underlying trust assets as far as IHT was concerned.

Under the new law such trusts will only be taxed as if the disabled person had a life interest if it was made in a will.

If it was lifetime creation then it would be taxed as if it was a discretionary trust.

So, a life interest trust for a disabled person will be taxed as if it was an immediate post death interest even if it was made during the lifetime of the settlor. The disabled person is deemed to own all the underlying trust assets and so the settlor will be deemed to have made a PET, and there will not be any 10-yearly or principal charges to IHT exit or proportionate charges.

Under the earlier law, a person who knew that he or she was going to become a disabled person could not create a trust for a disabled person for himself or herself. Now they can. Self settlement will also be permitted provided that the property is held on trusts:

1. Under which during the life of the disabled person no interest in possession in the settled property subsists;

2. If any of the trust property is applied during the life of the disabled person then it must be applied for the benefit of the disabled person;

3. If there is any power to bring the trusts to an end during the life of the disabled person, if such power is exercised:

    (i) the disabled person or another person will, on the trusts being brought to an end, be absolutely entitled to the settled property, or

    (ii) on the trusts being brought to an end, a disabled person's interest within s 89B(1)(a) or (c) will subsist in the settled property.

So someone in the early stages of Alzheimer's disease who still retains mental capacity could create a trust for a disabled person. However, there must be no interest in possession, and if any of the assets are handed out, the disabled person must be entitled to everything. So, in effect, a self settlement will have to take the form of a discretionary trust with the settlor within the class of beneficiaries.

Example

T creates a discretionary trust either during T's lifetime or in a will.

The terms of the trust would have to require the trustees to apply one-half of the capital for the benefit of the disabled person, and there must be no interest in possession.

Trusts for bereaved minors

5.4 It has been very common for testators to give legacies to children or grandchildren contingent on attaining a certain age—18, 21, 25.

Strictly they should have been taxed as if they were trusts without an interest in possession or discretionary trusts.

This meant that IHT would have to be paid on their creation during someone's lifetime if the assets transferred were in excess of the NRB, or the NRB had been absorbed by another discretionary trust in the seven years prior to the one you are dealing with.

In addition there would be a charge to IHT every 10 years and also whenever any capital was paid out from the trust by the trustees.

Such trusts usually became accumulation and maintenance settlements, and received special treatment as far as IHT was concerned.

The special treatment was that if they were created in a lifetime settlement it was not a chargeable disposal for IHT purposes, but was treated as a PET.

If the accumulation and maintenance settlement was created in a will, then the normal rules for the taxation of an estate on death applied. IHT was payable if the death estate was large enough, or if the NRB had been absorbed by lifetime gifts.

However, once the accumulation and maintenance trust was going, there was no further charge to IHT. There were no 10-yearly or principal charges or exit or proportionate charges.

This special treatment will now only apply to trusts for bereaved minors.

In order for a trust to be treated as a trust for bereaved minors, the following conditions must be satisfied:

1. The property must be held on the statutory trusts for the benefit of a bereaved minors under ss 46 and 47(1) of the Administration of Estates Act 1925; or

2. Held on trusts of the benefit of a bereaved minor, and the following conditions are satisfied:

    (A) the trust must be established under the will of the deceased parent of the bereaved minor;

    (B) the trust must provide that the bereaved minor, if he has not done so before attaining the age of 18, will on attaining that age become absolutely entitled to the settled property, any income arising from it, and any income that has arisen from the property held in the trust for his benefit which has been accumulated before that time;

    (C) the trust must also provide that so long as the bereaved minor is living and under the age of 18, if any of the settled property is applied for the benefit of a beneficiary, it is applied for the benefit of the bereaved minor; and

    (D) the trust must also provide that so long as bereaved minor is living and under the age of 18 either the bereaved minor is entitled to all of the income (if there is any) arising from any of the settled property or no such income may be applied for the benefit of any other person.

A "bereaved minor" is defined as a person who has not yet attained the age of 18 and at least one of whose parents has died. A step-parent or a person with parental responsibility for the child is included in the definition of "parent".

Note the various conditions have to be satisfied before a trust will be treated as a trust for bereaved minors. The most important points are that it is only parents who can create such a trust. In addition, the trust must be in a will. Furthermore, the children must become absolutely entitled to everything in the trust on attaining the age of 18. This means that they must be entitled to all capital in the trust, and any accumulated income.

So, if grandparents create a trust for the benefit of grandchildren, it will be taxed as if it was a trust without an interest possession or subject to the relevant property regime.

It parents create a trust during their lifetime for the benefit of the children contingent on attaining the age of 18, then again it will be taxed as if it were a trust without an interest in possession or subject to the relevant property regime.

The statutory trusts which arise on intestacy qualify for the special treatment, provided the beneficiary is a bereaved minor, which means that one or both of the parents must be dead.

Example

T makes a will containing a gift to all my children contingent on them attaining the age of 18.

Amendments enacted by the government gave special treatment to trusts created for those between 18 and 25 years.

These are trusts where the contingency is attaining an age no greater than 25.

This means that if there is a gift to a bereaved minor contingent on them attaining an age between 18 and 25, there will be a charge to IHT when the child satisfies the contingency.

If the contingency is 25, the rate of tax will be a maximum of 4.2 per cent.

This treatment applies only to settlements created by parents for the benefit of their children. In addition, the settlement must be in a will. So it does not apply to settlements created by grandparents. But it does mean that parents can give assets to children contingent on them attaining the age of 25, and as long as the assets are within the NRB, there will not be any charge to tax when the children attain 25 and become entitled.

Summary

5.5   If a person creates a settlement in his lifetime, it will be taxed as if it was a trust without an interest in possession or subject to the relevant property regime unless it is a trust for a disabled person within the s 89.

The same would apply to wills.

All trusts created in wills will be taxed as if they were trusts without an interest in possession or subject to the relevant property regime unless they come within one of the three exemptions—a life interest trust where a beneficiary will be absolutely entitled on the termination of the life interest, or a trust for a disabled person, or a trust for a bereaved minor.

Capital gains tax

5.6   The changes to the IHT treatment of trusts have some knock-on effects as far as capital gains tax is concerned.

The main change is the availability of hold-over relief.

Normally, hold-over relief applies to a restricted class of business assets.

However, if you have a trust taxed as if it was a trust without an interest in possession as far as IHT is concerned, then hold-over relief is available whatever the nature of the assets.

Why are HMRC so generous?

The reason is that in addition to the charge for CGT, there might also be a charge to IHT.

It would be rather harsh to make taxpayers pay both taxes at the same time, and so the law says that hold-over relief can be claimed whatever the nature of the assets, if IHT is payable on the same transaction.

The two situations where there might be a charge both to IHT and CGT are the lifetime creation of any trust apart from a trust for a disabled person, and when a beneficiary becomes absolutely entitled to any assets under a trust apart from a trust for a disabled person, a trust for a bereaved minor or an immediate post death interest.

The beneficiary may become absolutely entitled either because the trustees exercise their powers and hand assets out to a beneficiary or a beneficiary becomes absolutely entitled under the terms of the trust.

If a settlor creates a trust in his lifetime, apart from a trust for a disabled person and transfers assets to the settlement, the settlor is deemed to dispose of those assets at market value on the day of the transfer. If those assets have increased in value, there will be a potential liability to capital gains tax on the increase in value. Hold-over relief will be available whatever the nature of the assets. It is not limited to business assets. It is the settlor's right to claim this—they do not have to get the trustees or HMRC to agree.

In addition, whenever the trustees hand out capital, or a beneficiary becomes absolutely entitled, there will be a deemed disposal at market value by the trustees of all the assets to which the beneficiary is absolutely entitled. However, if both the beneficiaries and the trustees agree, then any gain can be held over even if the beneficiary has become entitled to non-business assets unless the trust is within one of the three exemptions.

If it is a trust for a disabled person created during the settlor's lifetime, it will be taxed as if it was a trust with an interest in possession, and so hold-over relief will be restricted to business assets.

Note that hold-over relief cannot be claimed if the trust is a settlor interested trust—one where the beneficiaries include the settlor, the settlor's spouse or civil partner or the infant children of the settlor who are not married or in a civil partnership. This restriction on the availability of hold-over relief applies to all assets including business assets. It is unclear whether this restriction applies to deemed disposals by the trustees.

So, under the new regime, unlimited hold-over relief will be available for a trust which does not come within one of the exceptions unless it is a settlor interested trust.

Normally, when a life tenant dies, there is a free uplift to market value for capital gains tax purposes of all the assets in the trust. In effect, the slate is wiped clean as far as the next entitled person is concerned. This will only happen if you have the trust in an immediate post death interest. If the trust does not come within the three exemptions, when a life tenant dies, there will be a deemed disposal at market value of all the assets in the trust, and a gain will accrue to the trustees if the assets have increased in value since the trustees purchased them or since they were transferred to them.

So, if a settlor creates life interest trust in his lifetime, it will be taxed as if it was a discretionary trust or subject to the relevant property regime.

The trustees may have to pay CGT on the death of a life tenant.

However, because it is taxed as if it was a discretionary trust as far as IHT is concerned, hold-over relief is available whatever the nature of the assets if the trustees and the beneficiaries agree, unless it is a settlor interested trust.

If it is a trust for a disabled person, the disabled person may have a life interest or may be deemed to have an interest in possession in the trust assets. When the disabled person dies, if the disabled person has a life interest, there will be a free uplift to market value of all the assets in the trust for CGT purposes but, of course, they will be subject to IHT on the death of the disabled person. If the trust takes the form of a discretionary trust, then there will not be an uplift to market value on the death of the disabled person.

If there is a trust for a bereaved minor, then there will be a deemed disposal whenever a child satisfies the contingency. Unlimited hold-over relief is available provided it is possible to divide the assets between the beneficiaries.

Summary

5.7   If a trust is not a trust for the disabled, it will be possible to claim hold-over relief whatever the nature of the assets transferred to the trustees. It is not limited to business assets.

Hold-over relief is available whatever the nature of the assets when a beneficiary becomes absolutely entitled to any of the trust assets if the trust does not come within the three exemptions.

However, hold-over relief is not available if the trust is a settlor interested trust.

Income tax

5.8   The rules about income tax have not changed.

So, if it is a trust with an interest in possession, the trustees will only pay basic rate tax. When they pay the income to the beneficiary entitled to the interest in possession, the beneficiary will get a credit for the tax paid by the trustees so if the beneficiary is a higher rate taxpayer, the beneficiary will have to pay extra tax to HMRC. If the beneficiary is a basic rate taxpayer, and the income from the trusts does not push the beneficiary into the higher rate tax band, there is no further tax to pay. If the beneficiary does not have any income, then the beneficiary will be able to get a refund from HMRC.

If there is no beneficiary with an interest in possession, then the trustees will have to pay income tax at 40% on all income apart from dividend income and 32.5% on dividend income. If they pay the income to a member of the class of beneficiaries, then the beneficiary gets a credit for the tax paid by the trustees. So, if the beneficiary is already a higher rate taxpayer, then the beneficiary will not have to pay any more tax. If the beneficiary is a basic rate taxpayer or does not have any income, then they will get a refund of tax.

SUMMARY OF CHANGES FROM 22 MARCH 2006

All settlements apart from immediate post death interests, trusts for disabled persons, and trusts for bereaved minors, the relevant property regime

IHT

5.9

- Inter vivos—payable on creation—rate 20 per cent if in excess of NRB or NRB exhausted by other settlements;
- On death—payable if estate large enough;
- Ten-yearly or principal charge—6 per cent;
- Exit or proportionate charge.

CGT

5.10

- Inter vivos creation—deemed disposal by settlor;
- On death—no CGT;
- Disposals by trustees chargeable;
- Deemed disposal if beneficiary becomes absolutely entitled;
- Hold-over relief available whatever the nature of the assets unless it is a settlor interested trust.

Income tax

IF NO INTEREST IN POSSESSION

5.11   Rate applicable to trusts

- If income applied for benefit of beneficiary, beneficiary gets credit for tax paid by trustees.
- Might be a trust for a vulnerable person

IF INTEREST IN POSSESSION

5.12

- Trustees pay basic rate tax.
- Beneficiary gets credit for whatever tax has been paid by the trustees.

Immediate post death interests, trusts for disabled persons, and trusts for bereaved minors

Inheritance tax

5.13

- Trust for disabled person created inter vivos—PET;
- On death, IHT may be payable;
- Life tenant deemed to own underlying trust assets;

- Surrender of life interest by life tenant—PET;
- Death of life tenant—deemed disposal of trust assets.

CGT

5.14

- Inter vivos—deemed disposal by settlor
- On death—no CGT
- Chargeable on disposal by trustees
- Deemed disposal at MV when beneficiary becomes absolutely entitled otherwise than on death of life tenant

Income tax

IF NO INTEREST IN POSSESSION

5.15

- Rate applicable to trusts
- If income applied for benefit of beneficiary, beneficiary gets credit for tax paid by trustees
- Might be a trust for a vulnerable person

IF INTEREST IN POSSESSION

5.16

- Trustees pay basic rate tax.
- Beneficiary gets credit for whatever tax has been paid by the trustees.

RULES PRIOR TO 22 MARCH 2006

Interest in possession trusts

Inheritance tax

5.17

- If created *inter vivos*, it was a PET.

- If created on death, IHT may be payable.
- The life tenant is deemed to own the underlying trust assets.
- If the life tenant surrenders all or part of his life interest, it is a PET.
- On the death of the life tenant, there is a deemed disposal of the trust assets.

CGT

5.18

- If created *inter vivos*, there was a deemed disposal by the settlor.
- If created on death, no CGT is payable.
- CGT is chargeable on disposals by the trustees.
- There is a deemed disposal at market value when a beneficiary becomes absolutely entitled otherwise than on the death of the life tenant.
- Usually CGT is not chargeable on the death of a life tenant.

Income tax

5.19

- Trustees are liable at basic rate.
- The beneficiary is subject to income tax, but receives a credit for the tax paid by the trustees.

Trusts without an interest in possession

Inheritance tax

5.20

- If created *inter vivos*, IHT was payable on creation—the rate is 20% if in excess of the NRB or the NRB is exhausted by other settlements.
- On death, IHT was payable if the estate is large enough.
- There is a ten-yearly charge—6%.

- IHT is also payable on capital distributions—the exit or proportionate charge.

CGT

5.21

- If created *inter vivos*, there was a deemed disposal by the settlor.
- If created on death, no CGT is payable.
- CGT is chargeable on disposals by the trustees.
- There is a deemed disposal at market value when a beneficiary becomes absolutely entitled.

Income tax

5.22

- The trustees pay the rate applicable to trusts.
- If income is applied for the benefit of a beneficiary, the beneficiary receives a credit for the tax paid by the trustees.

EXISTING TRUSTS

5.23   If a beneficiary becomes absolutely entitled on the termination of a life interest, then the old regime applies.

This means that if the life tenant gives up the whole or part of the life interest, they will be deemed to make a PET in whatever part of the life interest they give up.

On the death of such a life tenant, they will be deemed to dispose of all the assets in the trust for IHT purposes, and so those assets will be aggregated with the life tenant's personal estate, and IHT will be payable on all the personal assets and the assets in the trust.

If the trust does not terminate when the life interest ends, then the continuing trust will be taxed as if it was a trust without an interest in possession and subject to the relevant property regime unless a transitional serial interest comes into existence.

In general terms a transitional serial interest is one where a life interest under a settlement created before 22 March 2006 terminates before 6 April

2008 and another life interest comes into existence, or where it terminates after 6 April 2008 and the spouse or civil partner of the life tenant is entitled to another life interest.

Existing accumulation and maintenance settlements where the beneficiary becomes absolutely entitled on attaining the age of 18 will be subject to the old regime.

If that is not the case, then they will be subject to the relevant property regime from 6 April 2008.

What is a position if the contingency is attaining an age greater than 18? If it is possible to modify the terms of the trust so that the beneficiaries become absolutely entitled at the age of 18 again the current IHT treatment will continue.

If this does not apply, the trust will be subject to the relevant property regime as from 6 April 2008. This means there will be 10-yearly or principal charges to IHT and exit or persiodic charges will apply.

ADVICE TO EXISTING TRUSTEES

5.24 It is going to be necessary to review existing trusts. What is the best advice to give to trustees of existing trusts?

They may decide to do nothing.

If it is a life interest trust and a beneficiary will be absolutely entitled on the termination of the life interest, then the old law still applies.

On the other hand, if the trust continues, then it will be taxed as if it was a discretionary trust and subject to the relevant property regime unless a transitional serial interest comes into existence.

As IHT is not payable on the death of the life tenant at 40 per cent, the trustees may prefer this option as the overall IHT bill may be lower. However, CGT will be payable on the death of the life tenant.

Another possibility is to break the trust up if it is going to be taxed as a discretionary trust. This would be a PET by the life tenant, and a deemed disposal at market value for CGT purposes.

Settlements created before 22 March 2006.

1. To A for life, then to B absolutely.

The old treatment will continue.

A will be deemed to own all the trust assets. So when A dies, A will be deemed to dispose of all the assets in the trust, and those assets will be aggregated with A's personal estate.

There will also be a free uplift to market value of all the assets in the trust.

2. To A for life, then to B for life, then to C absolutely.

As far as A is concerned, the treatment is the same as above.

A will be deemed to own all the trust assets so when A dies, A will be deemed to dispose of all the assets in the trust, and those assets will be aggregated with A's personal estate.

Unless a transitional serial interest comes into existence, then the trust will then be taxed as if it was a discretionary trust and subject to the relevant property regime.

This means that there will be a charge to IHT every 10 years, and also exit or proportionate charged whenever the trustees hand out any capital.

If a transitional serial interest comes into existence, then the trust will still be taxed as if it was an interest in possession trust.

So IHT will be payable on B's death, and there will be a free uplift to market value on the death of B for all the assets in the trust as far as CGT is concerned.

It will be a transitional serial interest if A dies before 6 April 2008, or if after that, A and B are married or civil partners.

With regard to accumulation and maintenance settlements, there is no problem if the contingency is attaining the age of 18.

If that is not the case then, the trust could be amended so that the beneficiaries become absolutely entitled on attaining the age of 18.

It will then continue to receive the special treatment.

It may also be possible to terminate the accumulation and maintenance settlement to avoid it being treated as if it was a trust without an interest in possession.

Settlement before 22 March 2006.

To all my grandchildren contingent on them attaining the age of 25.

This is an accumulation and maintenance settlement.

If all the grandchildren will attain the age of 25 before 6 April 2008, then it will continue to be taxed as if it was accumulation and maintenance settlement.

This means that there will be no 10-yearly charge to IHT and no charge to IHT when a beneficiary attains the age of 25.

If all the grandchildren will not attain the age of 25 before the 6 April 2008 then, if the trustees do nothing, it will be be subject to the relevant property regime as from that date.

If the trustees so wish, it may be possible to avoid this.

The trustees may have express powers to terminate the trust, and if these are exercised before 6 April 2008, then the trust will still be taxed as an accumulation and maintenance settlement.

If there are no express powers, it might be possible to make use of s 32 of the Trustee Act 1925 which authorises trustees to advance up to one-half of the capital to which a beneficiary is contingently entitled to that beneficiary.

Chapter 6

IHT on Creation of Trusts Apart from Immediate Post Death Interests, Trusts for Disabled Persons and Trusts for Bereaved Minors

The inheritance tax treatment considered in this chapter is the treatment since 22 march 2006. Prior to that date this treatment only applied to discretionary trusts.

IHT ON ONE LIFETIME TRUST APART FROM TRUSTS FOR DISABLED PERSONS

6.1   If a settlor creates a trust apart from a trust for disabled persons in his lifetime, then IHT may be payable. If the assets transferred do not exceed the nil rate band (NRB), no inheritance tax (IHT) will be payable. However, if the assets do exceed the NRB, the excess is chargeable to IHT at one half of the rate which applies on death—20 per cent.

Example

Assume NRB is £300,000.

J transfers £606,000 to the trustees of a trust which is not a trust for a disabled person.

Assuming J has not made any other lifetime transfers, deduct two years annual exemption from £606,000 = £600,000.

Deduct NRB of £300,000 = £300,000 taxable.

IHT at 20 per cent = £60,000.

DEATH OF THE SETTLOR WITHIN SEVEN YEARS OF THE CREATION OF A TRUST APART FROM A TRUST FOR A DISABLED PERSON

6.2   If the settlor dies within seven years of the creation of a trust apart from a trust for a disabled person, then the IHT must be recalculated using the rates in force at the date of death. However, taper relief may reduce the amount of tax payable. If the death rate calculation means more tax is payable, then it has to be paid, but the tax paid when the settlement was first created can be deducted. If the death rate calculation results in less tax, then there is no refund.

Example

Please refer to the previous example.

Assume that the NRB is always £300,000—although the rates in force at the date of death would be used.

J dies within four-and-a-half years of the creation of the trust.

IHT at 40% on £600,000 − £300,000 = £120,000.

Taper relief—only 60% of the tax is payable = £72,000.

As IHT of £60,000 was paid when the settlement was created, another £12,000 must be paid.

IHT WHERE SETTLOR HAS CREATED MORE THAN ONE TRUST APART FROM TRUSTS FOR DISABLED PERSONS

6.3   The principle of cumulation applies to these trusts. This means that you must add together the amounts transferred to trusts apart from trusts for disabled persons in the previous seven years to see if the NRB has been fully or partly extinguished. If the total amount transferred in the previous seven years to trustees of trusts apart from trusts for disabled persons exceeds the NRB, then IHT at 20 per cent is payable on the new trust. If the total amount is less, then a part of the NRB is still available to offset against the new trust.

Example

Assume NRB is £300,000.

K creates a trust which is not a trust for a disabled person, and transfers £500,000 to the trustees.

Two years later, he creates another trust which is not a trust for a disabled person.

In order to determine the rate of tax, the earlier trust would have had to be brought into account as it is within seven years of the second one.

The earlier trust has absorbed the NRB.

Therefore IHT at 20 per cent is payable on all the assets transferred to the later trust.

Example

Assume NRB is £300,000.

L creates a trust which is not a trust for a disabled person, and transfers £256,000 to the trustees.

Five years later, he creates another trust which is not a trust for a disabled person, and transfers £306,000 to the trustees.

In order to determine the rate of tax, the earlier trust must be brought into account as it is within seven years of death.

Assuming L has not made any other lifetime gifts, deduct two years annual exemption from that trust: £256,000 − £6,000 = £250,000.

This means that £250,000 of the NRB has been absorbed, leaving £50,000 of NRB of £300,000 unabsorbed to offset against the later trust.

Deduct two years annual exemption from the later trust, assuming that it is available: £306,000 − £6,000 = £300,000.

Deduct balance of NRB: £300,000 − £50,000 = £250,000 taxable at 20 per cent = £50,000.

RECALCULATION OF IHT ON DEATH WHERE THE SETTLOR HAS CREATED SEVERAL TRUSTS APART FROM TRUSTS FOR DISABLED PERSONS

6.4   This paragraph is concerned with the recalculation of IHT on death.

If the settlor has created several trusts apart from trusts for disabled persons over the years, and dies within seven years of the creation of one or more, it is necessary to recalculate the tax payable in respect of all those created within seven years of death.

In order to determine the rate of tax which applies—NRB or 40 per cent—it is necessary to add together all the trusts apart from trusts for disabled persons created by the settlor in the seven years prior to the creation of the one you are dealing with. This means that it may be necessary to go back 14 years to determine the rate of tax applying to a lifetime discretionary trust on death.

Example

M creates a trust which is not a trust for a disabled person in June 2006.

He creates another in May 2013.

He dies in April 2020.

The May 2013 trust was created within seven years of death, and so it will be necessary to recalculate IHT using death rates.

Any trusts created within seven years of May 2013 will have to be taken into account in order to determine if there is anything of the NRB left.

So the June 2006 trust will have to be taken into account in calculating the rate of IHT applicable to the May 2013 discretionary trust.

Example

Assume NRB is £300,000.

N creates a trust which is not a trust for a disabled person in 2007, and transfers £500,000 to the trustees.

He creates another trust which is not a trust for a disabled person in 2013, and transfers £456,000 to the trustees.

He dies in 2019.

The 2013 trust was created within seven years of death, and so it will be necessary to recalculate the IHT using death rates.

The 2007 trust must be brought into account in order to determine if the NRB has been exhausted as it is within seven years of the 2013 trust.

The NRB has been exhausted by the 2006 trust, and so IHT at 40% will be payable on the 2013 discretionary trust.

However, taper relief will apply—possibly only 20% of the IHT will be payable.

It will then be necessary to ascertain the IHT paid when the trust was created. If more was paid, then it will not be necessary to pay any more, but if less was paid, then it will be necessary to pay the difference.

It will not be necessary to recalculate the IHT on the 2006 discretionary trust as it was more than seven years before death.

RECALCULATION OF IHT ON DEATH WHERE THE SETTLOR HAS CREATED SEVERAL TRUSTS APART FROM TRUSTS FOR DISABLED PERSONS AND HAS ALSO MADE PETS

6.5   In recalculating the IHT, if a settlor has made potentially exempt transfers (PETs) and created trusts apart from trusts for disabled persons within seven years of death, the PETs within seven years of death and prior to the creation of the trust on which tax is being recalculated must be taken into account in determining the rate of tax—whether the NRB has been exhausted.

So if the settlor has created trusts apart from trusts for disabled persons and also made PETs, both have to be taken into account in determining the rate of tax when recalculating the IHT on trusts apart from trusts for disabled persons on death. Note that the PETs are not included when first calculating the IHT on the lifetime creation of such a trust. However, if the donor dies within seven years of the creation of such a trust, any PETs made prior to the creation of that trust and within seven years of death must be cumulated.

If the PET was made more than seven years before death, then it does not have to be included. Once seven years have elapsed from a PET, it can be ignored for IHT purposes.

Example

Assume NRB is £300,000.

O makes the following gifts:

- ten years before death PET: £300,000;
- six years before death PET: £400,000;
- three years before death creates a trust which is not a trust for a disabled person: £500,000.

It will be necessary to recalculate the IHT payable on the trust three years before death.

It is now necessary to determine the rate of tax.

The PET made ten years before death can be ignored, but the PET made six years before death must be brought into account. It has absorbed the NRB, and therefore the whole £500,000 will be subject to IHT at 40 per cent.

It will then be necessary to ascertain the IHT paid when the trust was created. If more was paid, then it will not be necessary to pay any more, but if less was paid, then it will be necessary to pay the difference.

Example

Assume NRB is £300,000.

P makes the following gifts:

- ten years before death creates a trust which is not a trust for a disabled person: £100,000.
- Eight years before death PET: £200,000.
- Six years before death creates a trust which is not a trust for a disabled person: £300,000.
- Five years before death PET: £400,000.

It will be necessary to calculate the IHT payable on the PET five years before death as it was within seven years of death.

It will also be necessary to recalculate the IHT payable on the trust six years before death.

The PET made eight years before death can be ignored as it was more than seven years before death.

In calculating the IHT payable on the PET made five years before death it is necessary to take into account both the trusts.

As far as the trust created six years before death is concerned, it will be necessary to take into account the trust created 10-years before death in order to determine the rate of tax.

SUMMARY

6.6

- IHT is payable on the lifetime creation of trusts apart from trusts for disabled persons.
- In order to determine the rate of tax, any other trusts apart from trusts for disabled persons created within the previous seven years must be added together.
- If the settlor dies within seven years of the creation of this type of trust, the IHT must be recalculated using death rates.
- Taper relief may reduce the amount of tax payable.

Chapter 7

IHT While Trust Subsists—All Trusts Apart from Immediate Post Death Interests, Trusts for Disabled Persons and Trusts for Bereaved Minors

The inheritance tax treatment considered in this chapter is the treatment since 22 March 2006. Prior to that date this treatment only applied to discretionary trusts

TEN-YEARLY OR PRINCIPAL CHARGE

7.1   Section 64 of the Inheritance Tax Act (IHTA) 1984 imposes a charge on 'relevant property', which is defined by s 58 as settled property in which no qualifying interest in possession subsists, on the tenth anniversary of the creation of the discretionary trust.

The value charged is the value of the relevant property comprised in the settlement less agricultural property relief and business property relief.

The settlement has its own cumulative total. This is the aggregate of:

(*a*)   the values transferred by any chargeable transfers made by the settlor in the period of seven years ending with the day on which the settlement commenced; and

(*b*)   the amounts on which any charges to tax are imposed under s 65 in respect of the settlement in the 10 years before the anniversary concerned.

(*c*)   the value immediately after it became comprised in the settlement of any property which was not relevant property and has not subsequently become relevant property while remaining comprised in the settlement; and

(*d*)   the value, immediately after a related settlement commenced, of the property comprised in it.

Section 65 of the IHTA 1984 imposes a charge to Inheritance Tax (IHT) when property leaves the settlement; this is considered at **7.5** below.

The rate of tax is 30% of the rate which would be charged on a lifetime transfer. As the current lifetime rate is 20%, the rate of tax is therefore 6% once the nil rate band (NRB) has been exhausted.

TEN-YEARLY OR PRINCIPAL CHARGE WHERE THE SETTLOR HAS CREATED ONLY ONE TRUST

7.2   The first stage in the calculation is that all the property that is the subject of the settlement must be valued on the tenth anniversary of its creation and every subsequent tenth anniversary.

Assuming that there have been no other lifetime chargeable transfers, no payments from capital, no property which is not relevant property and no related settlement, the rate of tax is 6 per cent once the NRB has been exhausted. Lifetime chargeable transfers are transfers to trusts apart from trusts for disabled persons and also potentially exempt transfers (PETs) which have become chargeable because the settlor has died within seven years of the PET.

Example

Assume that the NRB has always been and will always be £300,000, that the assets transferred to the settlement do not increase in value, although in practice the NRB for the tax year in which the tenth anniversary falls would be used that there is no property in the settlement other than this relevant property, and no related settlement.

In 2006, S transfers quoted shares worth £500,000 to trustees to hold on trust and to apply the income or capital for such of the spouse of S and S's children and grandchildren as they shall in their absolute discretion think fit.

Assuming that S has not created any other settlements, and there are no payments from capital, in 2016 the trustees will pay IHT at 6% on £500,000 − £300,000 = £12,000.

Average rate is:

$$\frac{12,000}{500,000} \times 100 = 2.4\%$$

Example

Assume that the NRB has always been and will always be £300,000, and that the assets transferred to the settlement do not increase in value.

S creates a discretionary trust, and transfers £200,000 to the trustees. There is no other property in the settlement, and no related settlement.

S does not create any other settlements, and there are no payments from capital.

As the property within the settlement is less than the NRB, no IHT will be payable.

TEN-YEARLY OR PRINCIPAL CHARGES WHERE THE SETTLOR HAS CREATED OTHER TRUSTS APART FROM TRUSTS FOR DISABLED PERSONS

7.3   If the settlor has created more than one trust apart from trusts for disabled persons, any trusts apart from trusts for disabled persons within seven years of the trust which has a 10 year anniversary must be cumulated or totalled in order to see if the NRB has been exhausted. If the previous trust was created before 22 March 2006, it only needs to be cumulated if it is a discretionary trust. If the settlor is dead, failed PETs must also be cumulated.

Example

Assume that the NRB has always been and will always be £300,000, and that the values in each settlement do not change. In addition there are no other assets in the settlement, no related settlement.

S transfers £500,000 to the trustees of a trust which is not a trust for a disabled person.

S creates a second trust which again is not a trust for a disabled person, six years later.

As far as the latter settlement is concerned, on the occasion of the first 10-yearly charge it will be necessary to value all the assets which are the subject of the trust on the tenth anniversary of the creation of the trust. The cumulative total is £500,000, being the amount transferred to the earlier trust. If the NRB is £300,000, it means that all the assets in the later trust will be chargeable at 6 per cent.

Example

Assume that the NRB has always been and will always be £300,000, and that the assets transferred to the settlement do not increase in value. There is no other property in the settlement, no related settlement and the settlor is still alive.

U creates the following trusts which are not trusts for disabled persons:

2006   £200,000
2007   £300,000
2008   £500,000

The 2008 settlement has a cumulative total—the 2006 and 2007 settlements = £500,000. Assuming that on the second tenth anniversary the NRB is £300,000, then it will be absorbed by the 2006 and 2007 settlements. Accordingly, IHT at 6 per cent will be payable on the £500,000, assuming that those assets have not increased in value.

2007 settlement: the 2006 settlement has absorbed £200,000 of NRB, leaving £100,000 unabsorbed. £200,000 of the 2007 settlement is therefore taxable at 6 per cent.

TEN-YEARLY CHARGES WHERE THERE HAVE BEEN CAPITAL DISTRIBUTIONS IN THE PREVIOUS 10 YEARS

7.4   In calculating the 10-yearly charge, any capital distributions in the 10 years leading up to the 10-year anniversary must also be taken into account in determining the rate of tax.

Example

Assume that the NRB has always been and will always be £300,000, and that the values in each settlement do not change. There is no other property in the settlements, no related settlements and the settlor is still alive.

S transfers £250,000 to the trustees of a trust which is not a trust for a disabled person, in 2006.

S creates a second trust which is not a trust for a disabled person, in 2009.

The trustees of the 2009 settlement distribute £100,000 of the capital to a beneficiary in 2023.

The first 10-yearly charge for the 2009 trust will be in 2019; the cumulative capital will be the 2006 discretionary trust.

The second 10-yearly charge will be in 2029. The cumulative total will be the 2006 discretionary trust and the capital distribution in 2023. The NRB is clearly exhausted, and so the whole of the assets in the settlement in 2029 will be chargeable.

EXIT OR PROPORTIONATE CHARGES

7.5   There is also an exit or proportionate charge whenever the trustees distribute any capital, or a beneficiary becomes absolutely entitled to the assets in the trust.

The first stage in the calculation is to calculate the reduction in value of the assets in the trust. Usually this will be the same as the value of the assets distributed by the trustees.

The rate of tax is linked to the rate paid on the last 10-year anniversary; if the distribution is within the first 10 years, there must be a special calculation to determine the rate of tax.

It is also linked to the number of complete quarters which have elapsed since the last 10-year anniversary, or the creation of the trust.

Example

Assume that the NRB has always been and will always be £300,000, and that the assets transferred to the settlement do not increase in value.

In 2006, S transfers quoted shares worth £500,000 to trustees to hold on trust and to apply the income or capital for such of the spouse of S and S's children and grandchildren as they shall in their absolute discretion think fit.

Assuming that S has not created any other settlements or made any PETs, and there have been no payments from capital, in 2016 the trustees will pay IHT at 6% on £500,000 − £300,000 = £12,000.

Average rate is:

$$\frac{12,000}{500,000} \times 100 = 2.4\%$$

In 2022, the trustees transfer some of the shares to the grandchildren.

Thus, if five complete years have elapsed since the last 10-year anniversary, there are 20 quarters to be considered.

The rate of exit charge will therefore be 20/40 of the rate paid on the last 10-year anniversary.

The average rate is 2.4%.

So the exit charge will be 1.2%.

If the distribution is within the first 10 years, there is no previous 10-year anniversary on which to base the charge. In such a case, it is necessary to do a special calculation to determine the rate of tax.

The stages in the calculation are :

1. Calculate hypothetical transfer as per s 68(5)
   (i) the value of the property in the settlement immediately after it commenced, plus
   (ii) the value at the date of addition of any added property
   (iii) the value of property in a related settlement (value immediately after it commenced)
2. Add all chargeable transfers made by the settlor in seven years before date of settlement.

   Transfers on same day are ignored.

   If settlement created in will, other gifts ignored.
3. Deduct 2 from NRB.
4. Deduct balance of NRB, if any, from 1.
5. Calculate tax at 20%.
6. Convert into average rate for the settlement.
7. Calculate 30% of 6.
8. Calculate fall in value of fund
9. Calculate the number of quarters which have elapsed
10. Multiply $8 \times 7 \times \dfrac{9}{40}$

Example

T creates a settlement:

'To T1 and T2 my shares in A plc on trust to apply the income or capital for such of my children and grandchildren as they shall in their absolute discretion think fit'.

T has not made any other gifts or settlements.

The shares in A plc are worth £800,000.

Five years after the creation of the settlement, the trustees transfer half the shares (now worth £900,000) to the grandchildren. What IHT will be payable?

Assume that the NRB is £300,000.

The calculation is:

1. £800,000.
2. Nil.
3. £300,000.
4.   £800,000.
     $-$£300,000.
      £500,000.
5. 20% of £500, 000 = £100, 000.
6. $\dfrac{£100,000}{£800,000}$ = 12.50%.
7. 30% of 12.50% = 3.75%
8. £450,000.
9. 20.
10. £450, 000 × 3.75% × $\dfrac{20}{40}$

    = £8437.50.

SUMMARY

7.6

- IHT payable on creation whether it is a lifetime settlement or in a will.
- If the settlor dies within seven years of the creation of the settlement, then the IHT has to be recalculated using death rates.
- There is also a charge to IHT every 10 years.
- There is also a charge to IHT when capital leaves the trust.

Chapter 8

IHT on Immediate Post Death Interests

WHAT IS AN IMMEDIATE POST DEATH INTEREST?

8.1   These are described in more detail in **Chapter 5**, but in order for a trust to qualify as an immediate post death interest, the following conditions must be satisfied:

1. The settlement must be effected by will or under the law relating to intestacy.

2. The life tenant must have become beneficially entitled to the interest in possession on the death of the testator or intestate.

3. Section 71A does not apply to the property in which the interest subsists or the interest is not a disabled person's interest.

4. Condition 3 has been satisfied at all times since the life tenant became beneficially entitled to the interest in possession.

INHERITANCE TAX ON CREATION OF AN IMMEDIATE POST DEATH INTEREST

8.2   These settlements must be created by will, or arise under the intestacy rules, and so the normal rules about the taxation of estates on death apply. Inheritance Tax (IHT) will be payable if the estate is in excess of the nil rate band (NRB), or if the NRB has been absorbed by lifetime gifts in the seven years up to the date of death.

Example

Assume NRB is £300,000.

T, in his will, gives the whole of his estate to T1 and T2 to hold on trust for A for life, remainder to B.

On his death his estate is worth £1,000,000.

IHT will be payable on £1,000, 000 − NRB of £300,000 = £700,000 at 40% = £280,000.

If he had made an *inter vivos* gift of £350,000 five years before he died, the whole of his death estate would be taxable at 40 per cent.

There is no charge to IHT if the the life tenant is the spouse or civil partner of the settlor and is domiciled in the United Kingdom.

POSITION OF THE LIFE TENANT ENTITLED TO AN IMMEDIATE POST DEATH INTEREST

8.3   There is a fiction for IHT purposes that the life tenant owns all the trust assets. This fiction does not operate for other purposes. It follows from this that when the life tenant dies, for IHT purposes, the life tenant will be deemed to dispose of all the trust assets. The trust assets will be aggregated with the life tenant's personal estate, and any IHT will be apportioned between them.

If the trust assets comprise quoted shares worth £900,000, the life tenant will be deemed to own all the trust assets. So, when the life tenant dies, he will be deemed to dispose of all the trust assets. These assets will be aggregated with all the personal assets of the deceased, and the IHT payable will be calculated on the total. It must then be split between the trust assets and the personal assets in the proportion they bear to each other.

LIFETIME TERMINATIONS BY THE LIFE TENANT ENTITLED TO AN IMMEDIATE POST DEATH INTEREST

8.4   The fiction that the life tenant owns all the underlying trust assets also applies to lifetime terminations. If the life tenant surrenders or assigns all or part of his interest, then the life tenant will be deemed to make a potentially exempt transfer (PET) of whatever proportion of the underlying trust assets is surrendered, provided that the surrendered property is held:

- for one or more of the beneficiaries absolutely;
- on a trust for a disabled person.

No IHT will be payable if the life tenant survives for seven years—otherwise it will be.

If the life tenant sells his interest, he will be making a PET of the value of the trust assets less any consideration received for the life interest.

Example

S bequeaths shares worth £900,000 to trustees, T1 and T2, to hold on trust for A for life, remainder to B.

At all relevant times, shares are worth £900,000.

A sells his interest for £500,000.

A is deemed to have made a PET of £400,000.

However, an advancement to the life tenant will not normally result in a charge to IHT. The reason for that is that the life tenant is deemed to own the underlying trust assets.

If the life tenant surrenders his life interest to the remainderman, the trust is at an end, and there will be no charge to IHT as long as the life tenant lives for seven years after the surrender. If the life tenant transfers his interest to a person other than the remainderman person, that assignment will be a PET. There will also be a deemed disposal when the life tenant dies by the person entitled to the life interest.

POSITION OF THE REMAINDERMAN UNDER AN IMMEDIATE POST DEATH INTEREST

8.5   The fiction that the life tenant owns all the underlying trust assets means that the remainderman owns nothing for IHT purposes. So in the previous example, B owns nothing as far as IHT is concerned. B can do what he likes with his interest—for example, assign it to a child—and there will not be any IHT consequences whilst the life tenant is still living (for more detail see **8.6** below).

EXEMPTIONS AND RELIEFS

8.6

(*a*)   *IHT is not payable:* if the person whose interest in the property comes to an end becomes on the same occasion beneficially entitled to the property or to another interest in possession in the property (IHTA 1984, s 53(2)).

The fiction for IHT purposes is that the life tenant owns all the underlying trust assets. It follows from this that if the life tenant becomes absolutely entitled to the trust assets, no IHT will be payable—the life tenant already owns all the trust assets for IHT purposes. For trusts created after 22 March 2006 this only applies to immediate post death interests.

Example

Assume that this trust is created by will.

To A until he qualifies as a doctor, then to A and B.

B predeceases A before A qualifies.

A becomes absolutely entitled, but no IHT will be payable as A is already deemed to own the underlying assets.

Example

T1 and T2 are trustees of shares in Z plc which they purchased for £200,000. The shares are now worth £250,000.

They are about to exercise a power of advancement in favour of the life tenant, and vest all the shares in her.

This will not have any IHT consequences as the life tenant is deemed to own the underlying trust assets.

However, it will have CGT consequences (see **Chapter 11**).

(b) *Spouse or civil partner exemption:* If the settlement is created in a will, as the trustees are deemed to dispose of the trust assets at market value as the trust is now at an end and the life tenant is the spouse of the testator, again no IHT will be payable as long as the spouse is domiciled in the United Kingdom.

Similarly, if when the life tenant dies, the property passes to the spouse of the life tenant, no IHT will be payable. The position will be the same if instead of a spouse the life tenant is the civil partner of the testator, or the remainderman is the civil partner of the life tenant.

Example

S bequeaths assets to trustees, T1 and T2, to hold on trust for A for life, remainder to B.

If A is the spouse of the settlor, no IHT will be payable as long as A is domiciled in the United Kingdom.

If when A dies the property passes to B, and B is A's spouse, who is domiciled in the United Kingdom, no IHT will be payable.

A similar exemption now applies to civil partners.

(c) *Gifts of excluded property:* A legacy of excluded property to the trustees of a settlement will not incur any charge to IHT.

Excluded property is:

- property situated outside the United Kingdom if the person beneficially entitled to it is an individual domiciled outside the United Kingdom;

- a reversionary interest unless (a) it has at any time been acquired (whether by the person entitled to it or by a person previously entitled to it) for a consideration in money or money's worth, or (b) it is one to which the settlor or his spouse or civil partner has been beneficially entitled (IHTA 1984, s 48(1)).

If the testator is domiciled outside the United Kingdom, and bequeaths property situated outside the United Kingdom to the trustees of the settlement, no IHT will be payable. Note both conditions must be satisfied—domicile and property must both be outside the United Kingdom. If the settlor is domiciled in the United Kingdom, and the property is situated abroad, IHT will be payable.

The fiction for IHT purposes is that the life tenant owns all the underlying trust assets. It follows from this that the remainderman can own nothing, and can assign his interest without any IHT consequences.

One exemption from this is if the remainderman has purchased his interest for a consideration. In these circumstances, then any bequest by the remainderman of his interest will be a transfer for IHT purposes.

Similarly, if the reversionary interest is one to which the testator or his spouse or civil partner is beneficially entitled, then any bequest of it will be a transfer of value for IHT purposes.

(d) *Business property relief and agricultural property relief:* If the testator owns property qualifying for business property or agricultural property relief, then it can be bequeathed to the trustees of the settlement, and, if it is business property which qualifies for 100 per cent relief, no IHT will be payable.

If a trustee is entitled to an interest in possession in the trust property as remuneration for his services, and that interest represents *reasonable remuneration*, there will be no IHT consequences check

(e) Compliance with an order under the *Inheritance (Provision for Family and Dependants) Act 1975*.

SUMMARY

8.7

- IHT is payable if the estate is large enough.
- The life tenant is deemed to own all the trust assets.
- On death, IHT is payable on all the trust assets.
- Lifetime termination by the life tenant is a PET.
- Reversionary interests are not subject to IHT.

Chapter 9

Capital Gains Tax

CALCULATION OF CAPITAL GAINS TAX

9.1   In order to calculate the gain, it is necessary to take the sale price, and deduct from it the initial expenditure, subsequent expenditure, and the costs of disposal and acquisition.

So if A buys a holiday home, and spends money on extending it, that expenditure, the initial cost and the incidental costs of acquisition and disposal are all deductible from the sale price in order to calculate the gain. After deducting any reliefs or exemptions, the gain is taxable as the top slice of the taxpayer's income. So if the taxpayer is a higher rate taxpayer, the gain will be taxed at 40 per cent.

Normally, capital gains tax (CGT) is payable on a gain made on a sale or a gift. However, it is also payable whenever a capital sum arises. If an asset is destroyed, a capital sum payable under an insurance policy will be chargeable. If a copyright is sold for a capital sum, that capital sum will be subject to CGT.

CGT ON LIFETIME GIFTS

9.2   There are two rules affecting donors—if a disposal is otherwise than by way of a bargain made at arm's length, then the donor is deemed to dispose of those assets at market value. There are also rules dealing with transactions between connected persons. Any transaction between connected persons will be deemed to be at market value, whatever the consideration inserted in the transfer.

There is quite a complicated definition of connected persons in the CGT legislation.

Spouses are connected to each other. They are also connected to their and each other's relatives. Relatives include direct ancestors and lineal descendants, but not lateral relatives. So it includes parents, grandparents, children and grandchildren, but not nephews and nieces. A person who controls a company is deemed to be connected with that company. Partners in a business are deemed to be connected with each other except in relation to bona fide commercial arrangements. A settlor is deemed to be connected with the trustees of a settlement he has created.

Any transaction not at arm's length or between connected persons will be deemed to be at market value.

Example

T purchases an asset for £50,000.

He gives it to U when its market value is £90,000.

T will be deemed to dispose of the asset at market value at the date of the gift, i.e. £90.000. This will be the position for two reasons—it is a gift at an undervalue, and also because U will probably be related to T—his child or grandchild.

CAPITAL GAINS TAX ON DEATH

9.3   On death, there is a deemed acquisition of all the assets of the deceased at market value, but as there is no deemed disposal no chargeable gain or allowable loss accrues to the personal representatives. If the personal representatives transfer an asset to a beneficiary, then the beneficiary is deemed to acquire that asset at market value as at the date of death.

Example

V dies leaving a will containing the following gifts:

- shares in A plc which he purchased for £90,000, but are worth £150,000 at the date of death, to X and Y his executors and trustees to hold on trust;
- shares in B plc which he purchased for £170,000, but are worth £150,000 at the date of death, to Z.

X and Y will be deemed to acquire both shareholdings at market value as at the date of death, so in the case of shares in A plc, X and Y will acquire them at £150,000.

At some point in the administration of the estate they will become trustees—in their capacity as trustees they will be deemed to acquire the assets at market value as at the date of death.

X and Y will be deemed to acquire the shares in B plc for £150,000. When the shares in B plc are transferred to Z, Z will acquire them for CGT purposes at the market value as at the date of death, i.e. £150,000.

CGT EXEMPTIONS AND RELIEFS

9.4   The reliefs are:

- taper relief;
- indexation;
- annual exemption;
- main residence exemption;
- hold-over relief;
- roll-over relief;
- transfers between spouses;
- loss relief.

Taper relief

9.5   Taper relief was introduced in 1998, and replaced indexation allowance. It distinguishes between business assets and non-business assets. It operates by reducing the chargeable gain by various percentages depending on the length of ownership.

The percentage reduction is much higher in the case of business assets than non-business assets.

Number of whole years in qualifying holding period	Rate of relief for business assets	Rate of relief for non-business assets
0	100	100
1	50	100
2	25	100
3	25	95
4	25	90
5	25	85
6	25	80
7	25	75
8	25	70
9	25	65
10	25	60

Example

D has owned business assets for 8 years.

D sells them, realising a gain of £100,000.

Only 25 per cent of the gain will be chargeable.

Note that if the asset was owned on 6 April 1998, the whole years are calculated according to tax years.

If the asset was acquired after that date, the whole years are calculated from the date of acquisition.

If it is a non-business asset which was owned on 17 March 1998, then the taxpayer gets a bonus year when calculating taper relief. This does not apply to business assets.

Indexation allowance

9.6   The indexation allowance was designed to eliminate gains due to inflation from any charge to CGT. It does not apply to assets acquired after April 1998. However, indexation allowance can still be claimed in respect of assets owned before April 1998, but only up to that month. So if the asset was acquired in 1999, indexation allowance will not apply. Taper relief can be claimed. If the asset was acquired in 1995, then indexation allowance can be claimed up to April 1998, but thereafter only taper relief can be claimed.

The annual exemption

9.7   Trustees are entitled to one-half of the exemption available to an individual. If the settlor creates more than one settlement, the exemption is divided between them with a minimum of 10 per cent of the annual exemption. The annual exemption available to an individual in 2007/2008 is £9,200.

Main residence exemption

9.8   Section 225 of the Taxation of Chargeable Gains Act 1992 provides that the main residence exemption is available if the main residence is settled property, and has been the only or main residence of a person entitled to occupy the property under the terms of the settlement. The exemption also applies if the trustees exercise a discretion and permit the beneficiary to occupy the property.

Hold-over or gifts relief

9.9   The effect of the relief is to reduce the donee's acquisition cost to that of the donor plus indexation and any other allowable expenditure. It does not operate as an exemption—all it does is to postpone the liability until the donee sells the asset. If the donee sells the asset, the donee can only deduct the initial cost, subsequent expenditure and indexation allowance where relevant.

The relief applies to a limited class of assets:

(i)   it is, or is an interest in, an asset used for the purposes of a trade, profession or vocation carried on by:

- the transferor, or
- his personal company, or
- a member of a trading group of which the holding company is his personal company; or

(ii)   it consists of shares or securities of a trading company, or of the holding company of a trading company, where:

- the shares or securities are not listed on a recognised Stock Exchange or the trading company or holding company is the transferor's personal company;

(iii)   agricultural property, or an interest in agricultural property, within the meaning of Ch. II of Pt V of the Inheritance Tax Act 1984;

(iv)   it is a chargeable transfer within the meaning of the Inheritance Tax Act 1984 (or would be but for s 19 of that Act) and is not a potentially exempt transfer (within the meaning of that Act);

(v)   it is an exempt transfer by virtue of ss 24, 27 or 30 of that Act.

'Personal company' in relation to an individual means a company the voting rights in which are exercisable as to not less than 5 per cent by that individual.

'Holding company', 'trading company' and 'trading group' have the meanings given by para 22 of Sch A1 to the Taxation of Chargeable Gains Act 1992.

Note that if the transfer is to the trustees of a trust subject to the relevant property regime or taxed for IHT purposes as a discretionary trust, then hold-over relief can be claimed whatever the nature of the asset. It is not limited to business assets. However, hold-over relief is not available under any circumstances if it is a settlor interested trust. A settlor interested trust is one where the settlor, settlor's spouse or civil partner or infant children who are not married or in a civil partnership are the beneficiaries or within the class of beneficiaries.

Roll-over relief

9.10 This is where some business assets are sold, and the proceeds reinvested in other business assets. Business assets are defined in the legislation. All it does is to postpone the liability until the replacement asset is sold.

Transfers between spouses

9.11 No CGT is payable on transfers between spouses provided they are living together. Instead, the donee spouse is deemed to have acquired the asset for whatever it cost the donor spouse to acquire the asset.

Example

S1 purchases an asset for £400,000, and spends £30,000 on improving it.

The asset is then transferred to S2.

No CGT is payable. Instead, S2 will be deemed to acquire it for £430,000.

Losses

9.12 A loss can be offset against a gain. So, if the taxpayer has both made a gain and incurred a loss, the loss can be offset against the gain. If the loss exceeds the gain, then there is no liability to CGT.

What happens if the taxpayer has no gains in a tax year where a loss was incurred?

If the taxpayer has no gains in the tax year when the loss was incurred, the loss can be offset against other gains in future years. What cannot be done with a loss is to carry it back so as to set it off against gains made in previous years. There is one exception to the rule that losses cannot be carried back—if the taxpayer has died. Obviously the loss cannot be carried forward then.

The annual exemption cannot be claimed in the tax year in which the loss was incurred. However, if the loss is carried forward, then the annual exemption can be claimed in subsequent years.

Taper relief is applied once the gain has been reduced by any loss.

Example

Year 1: M incurrs a loss of £30,000.

M also makes a gain of £9,000.

The gain is wiped out, but the annual exemption is lost. There is a loss of £21,000 to carry forward.

Year 2: M makes a gain of £20,000.

The annual exemption can be claimed first. The loss carried forward absorbs the gain, leaving an unrelieved loss to carry forward.

Year 3: M makes a gain of £60,000.

The annual exemption can be claimed first, but the loss is clearly extinguished.

Note that there are restrictions on the use of losses on a transfer to trustees of a settlement and on a deemed disposal by trustees. A loss on a transfer to trustees of a settlement can only be set against a gain on a disposal to the same settlement. A loss on a deemed disposal by trustees can be offset against gains made by the trustees in the same tax year and prior to the disposal or on the same day; if there are no gains, the beneficiary can use the loss, but only on a disposal of the trust assets.

So, if a settlor transfers quoted shares to the trustees of a settlement, and the market value at the date of transfer is less than the purchase price paid by the settlor, then the settlor cannot offset that loss against a gain made on a sale of another asset. The loss can only be offset against a gain made on a notional disposal to the same settlement.

If a beneficiary becomes absolutely entitled in circumstances where there is a deemed disposal by the trustees, then if that disposal results in a loss, the loss can be offset against any gains the trustees have in the same tax year and prior to the disposal or on the same day. If there are no such gains, then the beneficiary can take over the loss, but the loss can only be offset against a gain made on a disposal of the trust assets.

SUMMARY

9.13

CGT on lifetime gifts:

- A donor will be deemed to dispose of all assets transferred at market value.

CGT on death:

- No CGT is usually payable on death.

Various reliefs may reduce or eliminate the liability, for example indexation and the annual exemption.

Chapter 10

CGT on Trusts apart from Immediate Post Death Interests, Trusts for Bereaved Minors and Trusts for Disabled Persons

CGT ON THE LIFETIME CREATION OF TRUSTS APART FROM IMMEDIATE POST DEATH INTERESTS, TRUSTS FOR BEREAVED MINORS AND TRUSTS FOR DISABLED PERSONS

10.1   A transfer of chargeable assets to trustees is a chargeable disposal for CGT purposes. The transfer will be deemed to be at market value. Normally hold-over relief only applies to business assets, but if the settlor is creating a trust apart from a trust for a disabled person, hold-over relief applies to all assets unless it is a settlor interested trust. A settlor interested trust is one where the beneficiaries or class of beneficiaries includes the settlor, the settlor's spouse or civil partner or the infant children of the settlor who are not married or in a civil partnership.

Example

S acquires shares in Y plc for £400,000.

He transfers them to the trustees of a discretionary trust when they are worth £600,000.

S will be deemed to dispose of the shares at the market value at the date of transfer to the trustees of the settlement, and so there will be a raw gain of £200,000 before deducting any exemptions or reliefs. However, the gain of £200,000 can be held over provided it is not a settlor interested trust. If the trustees later sell the shares, then the gain of £200,000 will be chargeable, along with any other gain made by the trustees.

Note that any loss made on the creation of the settlement can only be offset against gains made on another disposal to the same settlement.

Example

S acquires shares in A plc for £200,000.

He transfers them to the trustees of a settlement; at the date of transfer they are worth £150,000.

He sells shares in B plc, and makes a profit of £100,000.

He transfers shares in C plc to the trustees of the same settlement; at the date of transfer they are worth £400,000, but were purchased by S for £300,000.

S has made a loss on the transfer of shares in A plc to the trustees. He cannot offset it against the profit on the sale of shares in B plc. The loss can only be offset against a profit made on another transfer to the same settlement, and can be offset against the notional gain made on the transfer of shares in C plc. Note that special rules apply if the trust is settlor interested.

CGT ON THE CREATION BY WILL OF TRUSTS

10.2   If the settlement is created in a will, then the normal rules for CGT apply. No CGT is usually payable on death—instead there is a free uplift to market value. So the trustees will be deemed to acquire the assets at market value at the date of death.

DISPOSALS BY TRUSTEES

10.3   Disposals by trustees are chargeable. If the trustees sell assets, and make a gain, CGT will be payable at 40 per cent on the gain after allowing for any exemptions or reliefs.

CHARGE WHEN A BENEFICIARY BECOMES ABSOLUTELY ENTITLED UNDER A TRUST APART FROM IMMEDIATE POST DEATH INTERESTS, TRUSTS FOR BEREAVED MINORS AND TRUSTS FOR DISABLED PERSONS

10.4   If property is advanced to beneficiaries, or a beneficiary becomes absolutely entitled under the terms of the trust, there is a deemed disposal by the trustees.

Hold-over or gifts relief will be available whatever the nature of the assets unless it is a settlor interested trust.

So before parting with all the trust assets, the trustees should calculate the CGT liability, and ensure that they retain enough to meet that liability.

Example

T1 and T2 are trustees of a discretionary trust.

The trust deed provides that it must terminate at the expiry of 21 years when the children of the settlor become entitled to any undistributed capital or income.

All the income has been distributed.

There is one asset left in the trust—shares in G plc acquired by T1 and T2 for £800,000, but worth £900,000 on the 21st anniversary.

The trustees will be deemed to dispose of the shares in G plc for market value on the 21st anniversary.

There is a gain of £100,000, which will be chargeable to CGT at 40 per cent after allowing for any exemptions and reliefs.

However, the trustees and the children can agree that the gain should be held over, so CGT will only be payable when the children dispose of the shares. It is unclear whether hold-over relief is available if it is a settlor interested trust.

There are restrictions on what can be done with losses. If the deemed disposal at market value by the trustees when a beneficiary becomes absolutely entitled results in a notional loss, this has to be offset against a gain made on the disposal or other gains of the trustees in the same tax year but before the disposal. If they do not have any other gains, then it can be taken over by the beneficiary, but the beneficiary can only offset it against gains made on the disposal of the trust assets.

SUMMARY

10.5

- Lifetime creation is a disposal, but hold-over relief is available whether or not business assets have been transferred.
- No CGT is payable if the settlement is created by will.
- Disposals by trustees are chargeable.
- The advance of property to beneficiaries is a disposal at market value for CGT purposes.
- There is also a deemed disposal at market value whenever a beneficiary becomes absolutely entitled to the trust assets under the terms of the trust.
- Rate of tax is 40 per cent after deducting any exemptions or reliefs.

Chapter 11

CGT on Settlements—Immediate Post Death Interests, Trusts for Bereaved Minors and Trusts for Disabled Persons

LIFETIME CREATION OF TRUSTS FOR DISABLED PERSONS

11.1   The creation of a trust for a disabled person during the lifetime of the settlor is a chargeable disposal for capital gains tax purposes, although hold-over relief limited to business assets and taper relief may be available. A settlor is regarded as being connected with the trustees of any settlement created *inter vivos*. This means that the settlor will be deemed to dispose of any assets transferred to the trustees at market value.

Example

A purchases shares in A plc for £400,000.

He transfers them to the trustees of a trust for a disabled person.

At the date of transfer the shares are worth £500,000.

A will be deemed to dispose of the shares for £500,000—will be payable on £100,000 less any applicable reliefs and exemptions.

Note that any loss made on the creation of the settlement can only be offset against gains made on another disposal to the same settlement. Special rules apply if the trust is settlor interested.

Example

S acquires shares in A plc for £200,000.

He transfers them to the trustees of a trust for a disabled person; at the date of transfer they are worth £150,000.

He sells shares in B plc, and makes a profit of £100,000.

He transfers shares in C plc to the trustees of the same trust; at the date of transfer they are worth £400,000, but were purchased by S for £300,000.

S has made a loss on the transfer of shares in A plc to the trustees. He cannot offset it against the profit on the sale of shares in B plc. The loss can only be offset against a profit made on another transfer to the same trust, and can be offset against the notional gain made on the transfer of shares in C plc.

CREATION OF IMMEDIATE POST DEATH INTERESTS, TRUSTS FOR BEREAVED MINORS AND TRUSTS FOR DISABLED PERSONS BY WILL OR UNDER THE INTESTACY RULES

11.2   Immediate post death interests and trusts for bereaved minors can only be created by will or arise under the intestacy rules. Trusts for disabled persons can be created during the lifetime of the settlor and by will.

If the settlement is created by will, then the normal rule that CGT is not payable on death applies. Instead, the trustees will be deemed to acquire the assets at market value as at the date of death.

Example

A purchases shares in A plc for £400,000.

A gives them in his will to his executors and trustees to hold on trust for S for life, remainder to C.

At the date of A's death the shares are worth £500,000.

The executors/trustees will be deemed to acquire the shares for the value at the date of death, i.e. £500,000. In effect, the slate is wiped clean as far as CGT is concerned.

At some point, when the executors have finished administering the estate, they will become trustees. As trustees, they will be deemed to acquire the shares for the market value at the date of death, i.e. £500,000.

DISPOSALS BY TRUSTEES

11.3   Disposals by trustees are chargeable in accordance with normal principles.

With effect from 6 April 2004, the rate of tax payable by trustees of settlements with an interest in possession is 40 per cent.

Trustees are under a duty to review the trust investments periodically and take advice under the Trustee Act 2000, and probably will have to sell some. If they sell them for more than they acquired them for or purchased them for, then there is a possible charge to CGT. If the trustees do make a gain, it will be taxable at 40 per cent after deducting any relevant reliefs and exemptions.

Example

Please refer to the previous example.

If the trustees sell the shares in A plc for £600,000, they will be deemed to have made a gain of £100,000.

This will be taxable at 40 per cent after deducting any exemptions or reliefs.

IMMEDIATE POST DEATH INTERESTS AND CGT

11.4   The CGT implications of the creation of these trusts has been discussed earlier.

In the case of an immediate post death interest, there is a deemed disposal and re-acquisition by the trustees on the death of a beneficiary, but no chargeable gain or allowable loss accrues (s 72(1)).

Example

B and C are trustees of shares in Z plc holding them on trust for D for life, remainder to E under a trust created by will.

D dies.

The shares in Z plc are worth £500,000 at the date of D's death.

B and C will be deemed to dispose of the shares at market value as at the date of D's death—i.e. £500,000—but no chargeable gain will accrue to the trustees.

E will be deemed to acquire them at that value, i.e. £500,000.

Section 71(1) of the TCGA 1992 provides that when a person becomes absolutely entitled to any settled property as against the trustee, all the assets forming part of the settled property to which he becomes so entitled shall be deemed to have been disposed of by the trustee, and immediately re-acquired by him in his capacity as a trustee for a consideration equal to their market value. Under s 60(1) the deemed re-acquisition by the trustee is deemed to be by the beneficiary.

These provisions do not apply on death.

The effect of these sections is that when a beneficiary becomes absolutely entitled to settled property otherwise than on the death of a life tenant under an immediate post death interest, the trustees are deemed to dispose of the assets at market value. This may mean that the trustees are liable to capital gains tax. The beneficiary is deemed to acquire the assets at market value at the date when he became absolutely entitled to the settled property.

Hold-over or gifts relief can be claimed if it applies.

Trustees frequently have a power to advance the capital of a trust to the beneficiaries. If they advance assets forming part of the capital to a beneficiary, then there will be a deemed disposal by the trustees at market value of all the assets advanced to the beneficiary.

Example

Trustees of an immediate post death interest advance some of the trust assets to a beneficiary under a power in the settlement.

The trust assets advanced are shares in A plc now worth £200,000 but acquired or purchased by the trustees for £100,000.

The trustees will be deemed to have disposed of the shares at market value on the day when they are advanced to the beneficiary. There is a notional gain of £100,000, in the advancement of shares in A plc, and the trustees will have to pay the capital gains tax attributable to this.

Hold-over or gifts relief can be claimed if the transfer is of assets which qualify for that relief.

What happens if the deemed disposal results in a loss? Any loss must be offset against a gain made on the disposal to the beneficiary or gains made by the trustees in the same assessment year but before the disposal. If there are no such gains the loss can be transferred to the beneficiary, but it can only be offset against a gain made on a disposal of the trust assets, but not other assets.

Example

The trustees advance some of the trust assets to a beneficiary under a power in the settlement.

The trust assets advanced are shares in A plc now worth £200,000 but acquired or purchased by the trustees for £300,000.

The deemed disposal by the trustees will result in a loss of £100,000. The trustees must first offset this loss against any gain they have made in the tax year prior to the disposal. If there are no such gains, then the beneficiary, B, can take over the loss. However, B cannot offset the loss against any gains he makes on a disposal of non-trust assets. It must be offset against a gain made on a disposal of the trust assets.

Any provision introducing the assumption that assets are sold and immediately re-acquired does not imply that any expenditure is incurred as incidental to the sale or reacquisition. If there is a deemed disposal at market value, you cannot reduce any gain, or increase any loss by notional expenditure on the sale or reacquisition.

IMMEDIATE POST DEATH INTERESTS AND SUCCESSIVE LIFE INTERESTS

11.5   If the settlement continues after the death of the life tenant, there is a deemed acquisition by the trustees, but no disposal so chargeable gain accrues.

Example

A settlement created by will:

To A for life, then to B for life, then to C absolutely.

If B is not absolutely entitled, but instead has a life interest, on A's death there is a deemed disposal and re-acquisition by the trustees at market value, but again no chargeable gain accrues to the trustees. However, when B dies as he does not have an immediate post death interest, the trustees will be deemed to dispose of the assets in the trust, and if those assets have increased in value, then there will be a charge to CGT.

CGT AND TRUSTS FOR DISABLED PERSONS

11.6   The CGT consequences of the creation of this type of trust have already been discussed.

When the disabled person dies, if the trust takes the form of a life interest trust, then there will be a deemed disposal at market value, but no chargeable gain will accrue to the trustees.

However, if the trust takes the form of a discretionary trust, then there will not be a charge to capital gains tax when the disabled person dies. Instead, when the trustees distribute the assets in the trust, that will be a deemed disposal at market value of the assets the trustees distribute. If those assets have increased in value, then there will be a liability for capital gains tax.

TRUSTS FOR BEREAVED MINORS

11.7   When a child attains 18, there will be a deemed disposal at market value for capital gains tax purposes of all the assets in the trust to which the child is entitled. If those assets have increased in value, then there is a potential liability for capital gains tax on the trustees. However, if the trustees and child agree, then any gain can be held over whatever nature of the assets. This will only apply if the assets can be easily divided between the minors.

If the assets cannot be easily divided between the beneficiaries, then the disposal does not take place until the youngest beneficiary satisfies the contingency.

Example

T makes a will containing a gift to all my children contingent on them attaining the age of 18.

T has four children.

If the assets in the trust are quoted shares, then when each child attains 18, there will be a deemed disposal of one quarter of the shares, and if they have increased in value, there is a potential liability for CGT, but if the trustees and beneficiary agree, any gain can be held over.

On the other hand, if there is one asset in the trust, a house, which cannot be easily divided between the beneficiaries, then the deemed disposal at market value does not take place until the youngest child attains 18.

Hold-over relief is then limited to business assets as far as older children are concerned, but probably unrestricted hold-over relief is available as far as the youngest child's share is concerned.

DISPOSAL OF A BENEFICIAL INTEREST

11.8   Normally there will not be a charge to CGT on the disposal by a beneficiary of his interest in a settlement.

Example

Please refer to previous example.

If C assigns his interest, normally no CGT will be payable by C.

However, if the beneficiary has acquired his interest under the settlement for money or money's worth, then there will be a charge to capital gains tax if the consideration for the disposal is in excess of the purchase price of the interest, or if there is a gift element in the transfer, i.e. the market value is more than the purchase price.

Where a beneficiary disposes of an interest under a settlement for a consideration, and the settlor has an interest in the settlement, the trustees will be deemed to dispose of the assets and re-acquire them at market value.

Example

S creates a settlement:

To A for life, remainder to S.

If A disposes of his beneficial interest, then there will be a deemed disposal by the trustees of the trust assets at market value because S has an interest in the settlement.

Under anti-avoidance rules, S will have to bear the CGT liability.

SUMMARY

11.9

- Creation of an *inter vivos* settlement is a disposal for CGT purposes.
- No CGT is payable if the settlement is created in a will.
- Hold-over or gifts relief may be available.
- Trustees are liable for CGT on disposals of the trust assets.
- There is a charge to CGT when a beneficiary becomes absolutely entitled.
- There is no charge when the life tenant dies under an immediate post death interest or a trust for a disabled person where the disabled person has a life interest.
- Usually no CGT is chargeable when a beneficiary disposes of his/her beneficial interest.
- Various exemptions and reliefs may apply.

Chapter 12

Income Tax

INCOME TAX AND INTEREST IN POSSESSION TRUSTS

12.1   If there is an interest in possession, then trustees only pay basic rate tax. The trustees are not entitled to any personal allowance in their capacity as trustees. The beneficiary receives a credit for whatever tax has been paid by the trustees.

Thus, if the beneficiary is a basic rate taxpayer, and the income from the trust does not push him into the higher rate tax band, there will be no further tax liability. If he is already a higher rate taxpayer, then extra tax will have to be paid. If the beneficiary is a child, or has no income, then he will be entitled to a refund.

TRUSTEES' EXPENSES

12.2   The trustees will incur expenses in running the trust. They may have to pay the fees of accountants and solicitors, or, if they are themselves professionally qualified, there will be their own fees which has to be paid.

In calculating the tax liability of the trustees, they are not allowed to deduct management expenses in calculating the liability of the trustees for basic rate income tax. These have to be paid out of taxed income. This means that all the income paid to the trustees will not be paid to the beneficiary. The beneficiary will receive the income less the expenses. Accordingly, the beneficiary will not be able to obtain a full refund of income tax paid by the trustees if he is a lower rate taxpayer or does not pay tax because he has not received all the income paid to the trustees. Thus, if the beneficiary does not have much income, it is best if the expenses are paid out of capital in order to obtain a full refund of the tax paid by the trustees.

On the other hand, if the beneficiary is a higher rate taxpayer, then it is probably best if the expenses are paid out of income as it will reduce the income of that person.

Wills or lifetime settlements may give trustees a discretion as to whether the expenses are paid from income or capital; if that is not the case, then general principles of law will apply, and the trustees may have no discretion as to whether the expenses are paid from income or capital.

PAYMENTS FROM CAPITAL

12.3   Normally, income tax is not payable on payments to beneficiaries from capital, but it will be in the following situations:

(*a*)   where the payment is designed to augment income

(*b*)   the trust deed authorises the trustees to apply the capital to maintain a beneficiary in the same degree of comfort as he has enjoyed in the past;

(*c*)   the payments from capital amount to an annuity (*Revenue Law— Principles and Practice* (published by Tottel Publishing)).

INCOME TAX RATE APPLICABLE TO TRUSTS

12.4   Sections 479 and 480 of the Income Tax Act 2007 impose a charge on income in the case of settlements where there is a power to accumulate income or where the trustees have a discretion as to whether the income is distributed.

The expenses of the trust are deductible in computing the rate applicable to trusts.

The rate of tax is the rate applicable to trusts, which is 40% (32.5% in the case of dividends). Trustees of a discretionary trust in receipt of dividend income therefore have to pay an extra 22.5% in respect of the dividend; if it is interest paid by a bank or building society, then the trustees will have to pay a further 20% to HMRC as the bank or building society will usually deduct income tax at 20% before paying the interest to the trustees. The income tax paid by the trustees becomes a tax pool, and the trustees can offset any further tax which has to be paid against any tax left in the pool. Note that the first £1000 of income is taxed at the lower rate, savings rate or basic rate.

If the trustees pay the income to a beneficiary, then the beneficiary receives a credit for whatever has been paid by the trustees.

If the trustees distribute the dividend income to the beneficiaries, tax is charged at 40% on the grossed up amount of the dividend. The tax credit of 10% cannot be recovered.

If the trustees decide to retain the income, it will be treated as capital.

Example

Assume that the £1000 first slice has been absorbed by other income.

The trustees of a discretionary trust receive a net dividend of £1,800.

Tax of 10% will have been deducted from the gross dividend of £2,000. This is irrecoverable.

The trustees will have to pay tax at 32.5% on the gross dividend: £650 − £200 already paid = £450. The £450 paid by the trustees becomes part of a tax pool, and the trustees can offset any further tax payable against what remains in the tax pool.

If the trustees distribute the net sum, it will have to be grossed up at 40%.

$$£1,350 \times \frac{100}{60} = £2,250$$

The trustees will have to account to the HMRC for tax at 40% on £2,250 = £900 − £450 tax in the tax pool = £450.

The beneficiary will have a tax credit for £900.

Total tax	£200
Plus	£900
	£1,100

If the beneficiary is a higher rate taxpayer, it means that the rate of tax on the dividend is over 50%, whereas if the taxpayer had owned the shares personally, it would have been only 32.5%.

If the beneficiary is a lower or basic rate taxpayer, they will be able to recover the difference between basic rate and the 40% paid by the trustees on the grossed up amount.

22% of £2,250 is £495, so the basic rate taxpayer will recover £900 − £495 = £405.

Thus, a beneficiary who is a basic rate taxpayer will be paying tax of £695 on a dividend of £2,000, a percentage rate of 34.75 on the dividend, whereas if it had been paid to him directly the rate of tax would be 10%.

The 10% is irrecoverable.

Chapter 13

Trusts for Bereaved Minors

INHERITANCE TAX

13.1   It has been very common for testators to give legacies to children or grandchildren contingent on attaining a certain age—18, 21, 25. Strictly they should have been taxed as if they were trusts without an interest in possession or discretionary trusts. This meant that inheritance tax (IHT) would have to be paid on their creation during the settlor's lifetime if the assets transferred were in excess of the nil rate band (NRB), or the NRB had been absorbed by other discretionary trusts in the seven years prior to the current one. In addition there would be a charge to IHT every 10 years and also whenever any capital was paid out from the trust by the trustees. Such trusts usually became accumulation and maintenance settlements, and received special treatment as far as IHT was concerned. The special treatment was that if they were created in a lifetime settlement it was not a chargeable disposal for IHT purposes, but was treated as a PET. If the accumulation and maintenance settlement was created in a will, then the normal rules for the taxation of an estate on death applied. IHT was payable if the death estate was large enough, or if the NRB had been absorbed by lifetime gifts. However, once the accumulation and maintenance trust was going, there was no further charge to IHT. There were no 10-yearly charges or exit or proportionate charges.

This special treatment will now only apply to trusts for bereaved minors.

In order for a trust to be treated as a trust for bereaved minors, the following conditions must be satisfied:

1. The property must be held on the statutory trusts for the benefit of a bereaved minors under ss 46 and 47 (1) of the Administration of Estates Act 1925; or

2. Held on trusts of the benefit of a bereaved minor, and the following conditions are satisfied:

    (A) the trust must be established under the will of the deceased parent of the bereaved minor;

(B)   the trust must provide that the bereaved minor, if he has not done so before attaining the age of 18, will on attaining that age become absolutely entitled to the settled property, any income arising from it, and any income that has arisen from the property held in the trust for his benefit which has been accumulated before that time;

(C)   the trust must also provide that so long as bereaved minor is living and under the age of 18, if any of the settled property is applied for the benefit of a beneficiary, it is applied for the benefit of the bereaved minor, and

(D)   the trust must also provide that so long as bereaved minor is living and under the age of 18 either the bereaved minor is entitled to all of the income (if there is any) arising from any of the settled property or no such income may be applied for the benefit of any other person.

A "bereaved minor" is defined as a person who has not yet attained the age of 18 and at least one of whose parents has died. A step-parent and someone with parental responsibility for a child can also create such a settlement.

Various conditions have to be satisfied before a trust will be treated as a trust for bereaved minors. The most important points are that it is only parents who can create such a trust. In addition, the trust must be in a will. Furthermore, as the Finance Bill was originally drafted, the children had to become absolutely entitled to everything in the trust on attaining the age of 18.

So, if grandparents create a trust for the benefit of grandchildren, it will be subject to the relevant property regime.

If parents create a trust during their lifetime for the benefit of the children contingent on attaining the age of 18, then again it will be subject to the relevant property regime.

What about the statutory trusts which arise on intestacy? Do they qualify for the special treatment? The answer is yes, provided the beneficiary is a bereaved minor, which means that one or both of the parents must be dead.

Example

T makes a will containing a gift to all my children contingent on them attaining the age of 18.

This would be a trust for a bereaved minor as it is made in a will by a parent on his or her children. IHT will be payable on the death of T if T's estate in large enough, or the NRB has been absorbed by other gifts in the seven years prior to the death of T. However, no IHT will be payable when each child attains 18, and there will not be any 10-yearly or principal charge to IHT.

Amendments enacted by the government gave special treatment to 18—25 trusts. These are trusts where the contingency is attaining the age of 25. This means that if there is a gift to a bereaved minor contingent on them attaining the age of 25, there will be a charge to IHT when the child attains 25. The rate of tax will be a maximum of 4.2 per cent in so far as the assets are in excess of the NRB.

HMRC have made the point that many trusts for children and grandchildren contingent on the children attaining 25 will not be affected by these rules because the assets are within the NRB.

Grandparents can create trusts for grandchildren contingent on them attaining the age of 25, and as long as the assets in the trust are worth less than the NRB, there will be no 10-yearly charges or exit charges.

HOLD-OVER RELIEF ON TRUSTS FOR BEREAVED MINORS

13.2   Hold-over relief is available whatever the nature of the assets when a minor attains 18 or 25.

When a child attains 18 or an age between 18 and 25, there will be a deemed disposal at market value for capital gains tax (CGT) purposes of all the assets in the trust to which the child is entitled. If those assets have increased in value, then there is a potential liability for capital gains tax on the trustees.

However, if the trustees and child agree, then any gain can be held over whatever nature of the assets. This will only apply if the assets can be easily divided between the minors. If the assets cannot be easily divided between the beneficiaries, then the disposal does not take place until the youngest beneficiary satisfies the contingency.

Example

T makes a will containing a gift to all my children contingent on them attaining the age of 18.

T has four children.

If the assets in the trust are quoted shares, then when each child attains 18, there will be a deemed disposal of one quarter of the shares, and if they have increased in value, there is a potential liability for CGT, but if the trustees and beneficiary agree, any gain can be held over.

On the other hand, if there is one asset in the trust, a house, then the deemed disposal at market value does not take place until the youngest child attains 18.

Hold-over relief is then limited to business assets as far as older children are concerned, but probably unrestricted hold-over relief is available as far as the youngest child's share is concerned.

Similar rules apply to 18—25 trusts.

INCOME TAX

13.3 Trustees are liable at the rate applicable to trusts. If the income is applied for the maintenance, education and benefit of the beneficiary, the beneficiary receives a credit for the tax paid by the trustees.

If s 31 of the Trustee Act 1925 applies, the trustees will have to pay the income to a beneficiary on attaining the age of 18. The trustees will then be liable to income tax at basic rate.

Example

'To all my children when they attain 25'.

Assume there are two children.

Assume also that s 31 of the Trustee Act 1925 applies—so each child will be entitled to the income on attaining 18.

Whilst both children are under 18, there is no one with an interest in possession, and so the trustees will pay tax at the rate applicable to trusts.

If the income is applied for the maintenance, education or benefit of a child, that child will be entitled to a tax credit. If the child has no other income, the child will be entitled to a refund of tax.

When the eldest child attains 18, and becomes entittled to an interest in possession, the trustees only have to pay income tax at basic rate on the income to which that child is entitled. However, the trustees will still be paying income tax at the special rate applicable to trusts on the other half of the income.

The trust may be a trust for a vulnerable person; these are discussed in the next paragraph.

TRUSTS FOR VULNERABLE PERSONS

13.4 Trusts for vulnerable persons will receive special treatment as far as CGT and income tax are concerned.

A vulnerable person is a disabled person or any relevant minor.

Section 39 Finance Act 2005 (FA 2005) defines a person as a relevant minor if:

(*a*)   he has not yet attained the age of 18, and

(*b*)   at least one of his parents has died.

So in order for a minor to qualify as a relevant person, one of their parents must be dead. If both parents are still alive, then these provisions have no application.

Section 35 of the FA 2005 provides that where property is held on trusts for the benefit of a relevant minor those trusts are qualifying trusts if they are:

(*a*)   statutory trusts for the relevant minor under ss 46 and 47(1) of the Administration of Estates Act 1925 (succession on intestacy and statutory trusts in favour of relatives of the intestate;

(*b*)   trusts established under the will of a deceased parent of the relevant minor where:

  (i)   the relevant minor will, on attaining the age of eighteen, become absolutely entitled to the property, any income arising from it and any income that has arisen from property held on the trusts for his benefit and been accumulated before that time,

  (ii)   that, until that time, for so long as the relevant minor is living, if any of the property is applied for the benefit of a beneficiary, it is applied for the benefit of the relevant minor, and

  (iii)   that until that time, for so long as the relevant minor is living, either:

    (*a*)   the relevant minor is entitled to all the income (if there is any) arising from any of the property, or

    (*b*)   no such income may be applied for the benefit of any other person.

As far as relevant minors are concerned, if one of their parents has died intestate or partially intestate, then if the deceased parent has left a large enough estate, or was not married at the time of death, then the children of the deceased will be entitled under the statutory trusts. They statutory trusts of course provide that before the children can take that they must attain the age of 18, or marry under that age. So if one of the parents of a minor has died intestate, and the minor is entitled under the statutory trusts, then that trust is a qualifying trust.

If the parent has died leaving the will creating a trust for the benefit of a minor, then three conditions must be satisfied before these provisions apply. The first provision is that the minor will, on attaining the age of 18, become absolutely entitled to the property. In addition, the minor must also, on attaining 18, become absolutely untitled to any income arising from the property, and also any accumulated income as well.

The second condition is that if any property is applied for the benefit of a beneficiary, it must be applied for the benefit of the relevant minor.

The third condition is that the minor is entitled to all the income if there is any arising from any of the property.

Alternatively, there must be a provision in the trust document that none of the income may be applied for the benefit of any other person.

Note that the trustees of a vulnerable person must make an election for these provisions to apply.

Income tax

Section 26 of the FA 2005 provides that the trustees liability to income-tax for the tax year is to be reduced by an amount equal to:

$$TQT I - VTQI$$

Section 27 of the FA 2005 provides that the purpose of s 26 of the TQTI is the amount of income-tax to which the trustees would be liable for the tax year in respect of the qualifying trust income were it not for the Act.

VTQI is an amount equal to TLV1 − TLV2.

TLV2 is the total amount of income-tax and capital gains tax to which the vulnerable person would be liable for the tax year if his income-tax liability were computed.

TLV1 is what it would be if the qualifying trust income arising or treated as arising to the trustees in the tax year in respect of which the trustees are liable to income-tax were income of the vulnerable person for the tax year.

Capital gains tax

As far as CGT is concerned, the provision is simpler. The gains are treated as being the gains of the vulnerable person. So if the trustees of a qualifying trust make a gain, the gain is taxed as if it had accrued to the vulnerable beneficiary. So instead of the trustees paying CGT at 40 per cent, then the gains will be taxed as the top slice of the vulnerable beneficiary's income. So if the beneficiary is a basic rate taxpayer, the gain will be taxed at basic rate.

The effect of these provisions is to assume that any income or capital gains has been paid to the vulnerable person. The liability of the trustees is then accumulated to that of the beneficiary; so the trustees pay whatever rate of income tax or capital gains tax the beneficiary would have paid.

ACCUMULATION AND MAINTENANCE SETTLEMENTS

13.5 Accumulation and maintenance settlements cannot be created now.

Accumulation and maintenance settlements received favourable treatment for IHT purposes—but not for capital gains tax or income tax purposes.

The special treatment for IHT purposes was that there were no exit charges or 10-yearly charges.

Section 71(4) of the Inheritance Tax Act 1984 prescribes the rules for accumulation and maintenance settlements. It provides that no tax is chargeable:

(a) on a beneficiary's becoming beneficially entitled to, or to an interest in possession in, settled property on or before attaining the specified age; or

(b) on the death of a beneficiary before attaining the specified age.

Section 71 provides that the following conditions must be satisfied before a settlement qualifies as an accumulation and maintenance settlement:

(a) one or more persons (in this section referred to as beneficiaries) will, on or before attaining a specified age not exceeding 25, become beneficially entitled to the settled property or to an interest in possession in it; and

(b) no interest in possession subsists in it and the income from it is to be accumulated so far as not applied for the maintenance, education or benefit of a beneficiary; and

(c) not more than 25 years have elapsed since the commencement of the settlement or, if it was later, since the time (or latest time) when the conditions stated in paragraphs (a) and (b) above became satisfied with respect to the property; or

(d) all the persons who are or have been beneficiaries are or were either:

    (i) grandchildren of a common grandparent; or

    (ii) children, widows or widowers of such grandchildren who where themselves beneficiaries but died before the time when, had they survived, they would have become entitled as mentioned in (a) above.

CAPITAL GAINS TAX AND ACCUMULATION AND MAINTENANCE SETTLEMENTS

13.6   Hold-over relief is available for business assets when assets leave the trust, and if a beneficiary is not already entitled to an interest in possession, hold-over relief is available for all assets—it is not limited to business assets.

Example

'To all my grandchildren when they attain 25'.

When each grandchild attains 25, he or she will become entitled to a proportion of the assets. There will not be any charge to IHT, but there will be a deemed disposal at market value by trustees of all the assets the grandchild has become entitled to, as long as it is possible to split the assets. If it is not possible to split the assets, then the deemed disposal will take place when the youngest grandchild satisfies the contingency.

Hold-over relief, whatever the nature of the assets, will be available as long as the grandchildren have not acquired an interest in possession. If s 31 of the Trustee Act 1925 applies to this gift, then the grandchildren will have become entitled to the income at the age of 18, and thus will have obtained an interest in possession at the age of 18, and hold-over relief will be limited to business assets.

INCOME TAX AND ACCUMULATION AND MAINTENANCE SETTLEMENTS

13.7   Trustees are liable at the rate applicable to trusts. If the income is applied for the maintenance, education and benefit of the beneficiary, the beneficiary receives a credit for the tax paid by the trustees.

If s 31 of the Trustee Act 1925 applies, the trustees will have to pay the income to a beneficiary on attaining the age of 18. The trustees will then be liable to income tax at basic rate.

Example

'To all my grandchildren when they attain 25'.

Assume there are two grandchildren.

Assume also that s 31 of the Trustee Act 1925 applies—so each grandchild will be entitled to the income on attaining 18.

Whilst both grandchildren are under 18, there is no one with an interest in possession, and so the trustees will pay tax at the rate applicable to trusts.

If the income is applied for the maintenance, education or benefit of a grandchild, that grandchild will be entitled to a tax credit. If the grandchild has no other income, the grandchild will be entitled to a refund of tax.

If s 31 of the Trustee Act 1925 applies, a grandchild will be entitled to the income when he attains 18. The trustees will pay basic rate of tax on the income to which that child is entitled, and the grandchild will receive a tax credit for that tax.

TRANSITIONAL PROVISIONS WITH REGARD TO ACCUMULATION AND MAINTENANCE SETTLEMENTS

13.8 Existing accumulation and maintenance settlements where the beneficiary becomes absolutely entitled on attaining the age of 18 will be subject to the old regime. They will also be treated as accumulation and maintenance settlements if the beneficiaries become absolutely entitled before 6 April 2008.

If that is not the case, then they will be taxed as if they were trusts without an interest in possession from 6 April 2008 unless they are 18—25 trusts and the following conditions inter alia are satisfied:

1. The property must be held on trust for the benefit of a person who has not yet attained 25.

2. At least one of the person's parents has died.

3. The trust must have been established under the will of a deceased parent of the person.

4. The person will, on attaining the age of 25, if he has not done so will on attaining that age become absolutely entitled to the settled property, any income arising from it and any income that has arisen from the property held on the trusts for his benefit has been accumulated before that time.

5. If an accumulation and maintenance was in existence before 22 March 2006 and ceases to be one before 6 April 2008, if the property continues to be settled property and is held on trusts for the benefit of a person who has not yet attained 25, then it is treated as if it was an 18—25 trust as long as condition 4 is satisfied.

SUMMARY

13.9

- Trust for bereaved minors receive special treatment as far as IHT is concerned, but not with regard to CGT apart from the availability of hold-over relief or income tax.

- Trusts for bereaved minors can arise under the intestacy rules or can be created by parents in wills for the benefit of their own children.

- There are no exit charges or 10-yearly charges.

- Hold-over relief, whatever the nature of the assets, may be available when a child satisfies the contingency.

- Trustees will pay income tax at the special rate applicable to trusts whilst there is no child entitled to the income.

- The trust may be a trust for a vulnerable person and receive special treatment.

Chapter 14

Other Special Types of Trusts

BARE TRUSTS FOR MINORS

14.1   A bare trust for a minor may arise under a will where there is a gift to a beneficiary under the age of majority. An infant cannot give a valid receipt for the gift until the infant attains the age of 18, and it may be that the gift will have to be invested during the infancy of the beneficiary.

As far as inheritance tax (IHT) is concerned, if the infant dies under the age of 18, the trust property will form part of his death estate for IHT purposes. It is, of course, unlikely that the child's estate will be in excess of the nil rate band (NRB). If the infant attains 18, there will not be a deemed disposal.

The minor will also be taxed on any capital gain made by the trustees.

For income tax purposes, the income belongs to the minor, although the anti-avoidance rules discussed in **Chapter 15** may mean that the income is taxed as part of the settlor's income if there is a lifetime settlement in favour of infant children of the settlor who are not married or in a civil partnership.

PROTECTIVE TRUSTS

14.2   Protective trusts are where the beneficiary loses his or her interest if they become bankrupt or assign or charge their interest under the trust. Strictly, they should then be taxed as discretionary trusts, but they are treated as trusts with an interest in possession for IHT purposes. This means that there will not be any 10-yearly charges or exit charges, but IHT will be payable on the death of the beneficiary.

Section 88 of the Inheritance Tax Act 1984 applies to protective trusts created by will, and provides that for the purposes of the Inheritance Tax Act 1984, the failure or determination of the trusts specified in s 33(1)(i) of the Trustee Act 1925 shall be disregarded. It also provides that the principal beneficiary shall be treated as having an interest in possession in the property subject to the protective trust. If the protective trust is created during the lifetime of the settlor, then it is taxed as if was a discretionary trust.

However, there is no special treatment for CGT or income tax purposes, and so far as these taxes are concerned, these trusts will be taxed as if they were discretionary trusts or subject to the relevant property regime; for a discussion of their treatment, please see **Chapter 10**.

TRUSTS FOR DISABLED PERSONS

14.3   If a settlor creates a trust in his lifetime for a disabled person, and complies with the rules in s 89(4) of the Inheritance Tax Act 1984, then it will not be taxed as if it was a trust without an interest in possession or a discretionary trust; instead it will be taxed as if the disabled person had a life interest. This means that there will be no charge to IHT if the settlor creates one of these trusts during his or her lifetime. It will be a PET, and as long as the settlor survives for seven years, it will not have any adverse IHT consequences.

If the testator creates a trust for a disabled person in his will, then IHT will be payable on the death of the testator if the testator's estate is large enough, or the NRB has been absorbed by lifetime gifts in the seven years prior to death, in accordance with the normal rules about the taxation of estates on death.

However, there will not be any 10-yearly or exit or proportionate charges, but IHT may be payable on the death of the disabled person as the settled assets will be aggregated with the disabled person's personal assets.

Section 89(1) of the Inheritance Tax Act 1984 applies to settled property transferred into a settlement after 9 March 1981 and held on trusts:

(a)   under which, during the life of a disabled person, no interest in possession in the settled property subsists: and

(b)   which secure that not less than half of the settled property which is applied during his life is applied for his benefit.

Section 89(4) defines a disabled person as a person who, when the property was transferred into the settlement, was:

(a)   incapable by reason of mental disorder within the meaning of the Mental Health Act 1983, of administering his property or managing his own affairs; or

(b)   in receipt of an attendance allowance or disability living allowance by virtue of entitlement to the care component at the highest or middle rate.

Under s 89(2), the disabled person is treated as beneficially entitled to an interest in possession of the settled property.

The definition of a trust for a disabled person has also been extended so as to include trusts where the disabled person has a life interest. This was not necessary under the old law prior to 22 March 2006 as if a disabled person had a life interest, then the disabled person would be deemed to own the underlying trust assets as far as IHT was concerned. Under the new law such trusts will only be taxed as if the disabled person had a life interest if it was made in a will.

Self settlements by disabled persons will be taxed as if they were trusts with an interest in possession. The person will have to convince HMRC that he or she had a condition which meant that they were likely to become a disabled person.

As far as CGT is concerned, Sch 1 to the Taxation of Chargeable Gains Act 1992 provides that if settled property is held on trusts which secure that, during the lifetime of a mentally disabled person or a person in receipt of attendance allowance or a disability living allowance by virtue of entitlement to the care component at the highest or middle rate:

(*a*)   not less than half of the property which is applied is applied for the benefit of that person; and

(*b*)   that person is entitled to not less than half of the income arising from the property, or no such income may be applied for the benefit of any other person, the annual exemption available to individuals will be available in full to the trustees.

Thus, as far as CGT is concerned, the concession is of a limited nature. Normally, the trustees of the settlement are only entitled to annual exemption equal to one half of that available to private individuals, but if the trust complies with the CGT rules for disabled trusts, then the full exemption is allowable.

TRUSTS FOR THE VULNERABLE PERSONS

14.4   A vulnerable person is a disabled person or any relevant minor. A disabled person is defined in s 38(1) of the Finance Act 2005 as:

(*a*)   a person who by reason of mental disorder within the meaning of the Mental Health Act 1983 is incapable of administering his property or managing his affairs; or

(*b*)   a person is in receipt of attendance allowance or of disability living allowance by virtue of entitlement to the care component at the highest middle rate.

Section 38(2) provides that a person is to be treated as a disabled person under subsection (1) (a) if he satisfies the HMRC:

(a) that if he were to meet the prescribed conditions as to residence under s 64 (1) of SSCBA 1992 or s 64(1) of SSCBA(NI)A 1992 he would be entitled to receive attendance allowance; or

(b) that if he were to meet the prescribed conditions as to residence under s 71(6) of SSBCA 1992 or s 71(6) of SSCB(NI)A 1992 he would be entitled to receive disability living allowance by virtue of entitlement to the care component at the highest or middle rate.

Section 34(2) provides that the qualifying conditions for a trust for a disabled person are:

(a) that if any of the property is applied for the benefit of a beneficiary, it is applied for the benefit of the disabled person; and

(b) either that the disabled person is entitled to all the income (if there is any) arising from any of the property or that no such income may be applied for the benefit of any other person.

This does not mean that the disabled person must be entitled to the income and the property in the trust. What it means is that during the life of the disabled person, or until the trust is terminated, if the trustees advance any of the property in the trust, then the disabled person must be the only person for whose benefit it can be applied. In addition, the disabled person must be entitled to the income, or alternatively no other person is entitled to the income.

What types of trust will be included? Clearly, a life interest trust where the disabled person was the life tenant will be included provided there is no express power of advancement in favour of the remainderman. The disabled person as the life tenant is the only person entitled to the income. During the lifetime of the life tenant the capital cannot be applied for the benefit of the remainderman. It does not matter that there might be a power to advance the capital to the life tenant—that satisfies paragraph (a), that if any of the property is applied for the benefit of a beneficiary it is applied for the benefit of the disabled person.

What about a discretionary trust? The disabled person could be within the class of beneficiaries together with other family members. However, the terms of the discretionary trust would have to provide that during the life of the disabled person both the property and the income must be applied for the benefit of the disabled person. This does not mean that the trustees of the discretionary trust have to pay out the income and the capital. They could decide to retain it. But the terms of the trust must be such that if they do decide to pay it out, then it must be paid to the disabled person.

In order for a trust to be treated as a trust for a vulnerable person, then the trustees must elect for this treatment.

Income tax

14.5   Section 26 provides that the trustees liability to income-tax for the tax year is to be reduced by an amount equal to:

$$TQT\ I - VTQI$$

Section 27 provides that the purpose of s 26 of the TQTI is the amount of income-tax to which the trustees would be liable for the tax year in respect of the qualifying trust income were it not for the Act.

VTQI is an amount equal to TLV1—TLV2.

TLV2 is the total amount of income-tax and capital gains tax to which the vulnerable person would be liable for the tax year if his income-tax liability were computed.

TLV1 is what it would be if the qualifying trust income arising or treated as arising to the trustees in the tax year in respect of which the trustees are liable to income-tax were income of the vulnerable person for the tax year.

Capital gains tax

14.6   As far as CGT is concerned, the provision is simpler. It is assumed that the gains of the trustees are taxed as the top slice of the income of the vulnerable person.

The effect of these provisions is to assume that any income or capital gains accruing to the trustees has been paid over to the vulnerable person, and to assimilate the liability of the trustees the liability of the beneficiary on this assumption.

SUMMARY

14.7   Bare trust for a minor—minor will own assets as far as IHT is concerned. Any income or capital gains accruing to the trustees will be taxed as belonging to the minor unless the anti-avoidance rules have been infringed.

The main beneficiary under a protective trust created by will will be treated as having an immediate post death interest.

A disabled person under a disabled persons trust will be treated as having an interest in possession in all the assets the subject of the trust.

Other Special Types of Trusts

If a trust for a vulnerable person exists, then if the conditions for such a trust are satisfied, then the trustees can elect to pay income tax and capital gains tax on the basis that the income and gains are taxed as if they were the top slice of the income of the vulnerable person.

Chapter 15

Anti-avoidance Provisions

INCOME TAX

15.1   As far as income tax is concerned, there are two types of anti-avoidance provision: one catching those settlements where the settlor retains an interest, the other catching settlements on infant children of the settlor who are not married or in a civil partnership. Settlements which benefit the settlor's spouse are also caught. If a trust falls foul of an anti-avoidance provision, the effect is that the income will be deemed to belong to the settlor rather than the beneficiary.

Settlor with an interest in a settlement

15.2   In general, a settlement must not benefit the settlor or the settlor's spouse or civil partner; if it does, the income will be deemed to belong to the settlor.

Section 624(1) of the Income Tax (Trading and other Income) Act 2005 provides that income arising under a settlement during the life of the settlor shall be treated as the income of the settlor unless the income arises from property in which the settlor has no interest.

Section 625(2) provides that a settlor shall be regarded as having an interest in property if that property or any related property is, or will or may become, payable to or applicable for the benefit of the settlor or his spouse or his civil partner.

Section 625(4) provides that the spouse or civil partner of the settlor does not include:

(a)   a spouse or civil partner from whom the settlor is separated under an order of a court or a separation agreement;

(b)   a spouse or civil partner from whom the settlor is separated where the separation is likely to be permanent;

(c)   the widow or widower or surviving civil partner of the settlor or (*d*)   a person to whom the settlor is not married but may later marry or a person of whom the settlor is not a civil partner but of whom the settlor may later be a civil partner.

Section 625(2) provides that a settlor shall not be regarded as having an interest in property if and so long as none of that property, and no related property, can become payable or applicable except in the event of:

(*a*)   the bankruptcy of some person who is or may become beneficially entitled to the property or any related property; or

(*b*)   an assignment of or charge on the property or any related property being made or given by some such person; or

(*c*)   the charging of the property or any related property by such a person;

(*d*)   in the case of a marriage settlement or civil partnership settlement, the death of both parties to the marriage or civil partnership and of all any of the children of the family of the parties to the marriage or civil partnership; and

(*e*)   the death of a child of the settlor who had become beneficially entitled to the property or any related property at an age not exceeding 25.

Section 625(3) provides that a settlor shall not be regarded as having an interest in property if there are no circumstances in which the property or any related property can become payable or applicable as mentioned in subsection (1) during the life of a person other than the bankruptcy of the person, or the assignment or charging of the person's interest in the property or any related property, and the person is alive and under 25 years of age.

Section 626 provides that the reference in subsection (1) to a settlement does not include an outright gift by one spouse to the other or one civil partner to the other of property from which income arises, unless:

(*a*)   the gift does not carry a right to the whole of that income; or

(*b*)   the property given is wholly or substantially a right to income.

A gift is not an outright gift if it is subject to conditions, or if the property given or any related property is or will or may become, in any circumstances whatsoever, payable to or applicable for the benefit of the donor.

Section 633 taxes capital payments to the settlor where there is undistributed income. The capital payment is regarded as income as far as it does not exceed undistributed income in any year of assessment, and any excess is treated as the income of the settlor in subsequent years of assessment, again up to the undistributed income.

The sum is grossed up at basic and additional rates, and the settlor is entitled to a credit for the tax, but he cannot obtain any repayment.

Section 634(1) defines capital sum as:

(i)   any sum paid by way of loan or repayment of a loan; and

(ii) any other sum paid otherwise as income being a sum which is not paid for full consideration in money or money's worth.

Thus, if the trustees make a loan to the settlor, and do not distribute the income, the payment will be regarded as income in so far as it does not exceed the undistributed income. The settlor will be taxed on the loan as if it was income up to the undistributed income.

Payment to infant children of the settlor who are not married or in a civil partnership

15.3   If the income from a settlement is more than £100, and is paid to the infant child of the settlor who is not married or in a civil partnership, it is taxed as the income of the settlor.

CAPITAL GAINS

Settlor with an interest in a settlement

15.4   Section 77(1) of the Taxation of Chargeable Gains Act 1992 provides that chargeable gains will be treated as accruing to the settlor in a year of assessment if the settlor has an interest in the settlement at any time during the year.

Section 77(2) provides that a settlor has an interest in a settlement if:

(i)   any property which may at any time be comprised in the settlement, or any derived property is, or will or may become, payable to or applicable for the benefit of the settlor or his spouse or civil partner in any circumstances whatsoever; or

(ii) the settlor or his spouse or civil partner enjoys a benefit deriving directly or indirectly from any property which is comprised in the settlement or any derived property.

Section 77 (2A) provides that a settlor shall also be regarded as having an interest in a settlement if any property which is or may at any time be comprised in the settlement, or any derived property is, or will or may become payable to or applicable for the benefit of a child of the settlor, at a time when that child is a dependent child of his, in any circumstances whatsoever, or a dependent child of the settlor enjoys a benefit deriving directly or indirectly from any property which is comprised in the settlement or any derived property. A 'dependent child' is defined as a child who is under the age of 18 years, unmarried and who does not have a civil partner. 'Child' also includes a stepchild.

The settlor can recover from the trustees any capital gains tax (CGT) paid, and can offset any losses incurred in a personal capacity against the gain. Losses incurred by the trustees cannot be taken over by the settlor.

Settlor-interested trusts and hold-over or gifts relief

15.5   Hold-over or gifts relief usually applies only to transfers of business assets, but if assets are transferred to the trustees of a discretionary trust, hold-over relief is available whatever the nature of the assets. The effect of hold-over relief is to postpone payment of the tax until the trustees sell or dispose or are deemed to dispose of the assets. However, hold-over relief is not available if it is a settlor-interested trust. This is defined as a trust where the settlor or the settlor's spouse or civil partnership or infant children who are not married or in a civil partnership can benefit either directly or indirectly.

There are also provisions for clawback which will apply if a settlement becomes a settlor-interested trust within six years of the end of the year of assessment in which the disposal was made.

Example

S1 owns shares in A Ltd which he purchased for £200,000.

He transfers the shares to the trustees of a trust:

- where S1 or his spouse is a beneficiary;
- where S1 or his spouse is within the class of discretionary beneficiaries;
- where S1 or his spouse is not a beneficiary, but they benefit indirectly from the trust assets;
- where S1 or S2 is not a beneficiary, but the trustees have power to add them as beneficiaries.

In the first two situations, hold-over relief will not be available as S1 and S2 are beneficiaries or within the class of beneficiaries.

How can settlors benefit indirectly from trust assets?

Assume that S1 transfers a house to the trustees of a discretionary trust, and claims hold-over relief on the transfer. S1 and his spouse, S2, are not within the class of beneficiaries. The trustees permit a child of S1 and S2 to live in the house. S1 and S2 also live there. S1 and S2 are receiving an indirect benefit, and the hold-over or gifts relief will be clawed back. This would only apply if S1 and S2 moved into the house within the clawback period, which applies if a settlement becomes a settlor-interested trust within six years after the end of the year of assessment in which the disposal was made.

In the last situation, when the trustees add either S1 or S2 as beneficiaries, then the hold-over relief will be clawed back and S1 will have to pay whatever CGT is due on the held over gain, provided that S1 or S2 are added as beneficiaries within six years of the end of the year of assessment in which the disposal was made.

IHT AND ASSOCIATED OPERATIONS

15.6   There are anti-avoidance rules contained in the Inheritance Tax Act 1984 which seek to nullify two or more transactions designed to reduce the value transferred or the IHT chargeable.

If the rules apply, then the effect is that the final disposal will be deemed to have been made by the original transferor.

Example

S1 is much wealthier than his spouse, S2.

S1 transfers assets to S2. No IHT is payable because of the spouse exemption.

S2 makes use of the *inter vivos* exemptions from IHT in order to transfer assets to the children.

If S1 gave the assets to S2 on condition that she made the gifts to the children, then the HMRC will argue that this was an associated operation, and therefore the gifts were really made by S1.

SUMMARY

15.7   A lifetime settlement which benefits the settlor, the settlor's spouse or civil partner or the infant children of the settlor who are not married or in a civil partnership will usually be caught by anti avoidance rules and any income or capital gains accruing to the trustees will be taxed as belonging to the settlor.

Chapter 16

When to Use Settlements and Which Type

LIFE INTEREST TRUST

16.1   When is it appropriate to use a life interest trust?

- *Where the parties have children from previous relationships, and wish to ensure those children benefit*

One obvious situation is where the testator has children from a previous relationship, and wishes to benefit those children. If that is the case, then all the testator can do to ensure that the children take ultimately is to give the surviving spouse or cohabitee a life interest with remainder to the children of the previous relationship. If that is done, then the testator can rest assured that he has done as much as possible to ensure that the children will take, although of course the surviving spouse or cohabitee may apply under the Inheritance (Provision for Family and Dependants) Act 1975 on the basis that the testator has not made reasonable financial provision for the survivor.

It is, of course, possible and probably desirable to empower the trustees to hand out the capital to the life tenant in case the income proves to be insufficient to provide for the needs of the surviving spouse. If the power is exercised, it may reduce the entitlement of the children at the end of the day, but it is probably unwise not to include such powers. Frequently, the testator will not have many assets beyond the house or a share in the house. In that case, the best advice may be to give the surviving spouse or cohabitee a life interest in the house, with an absolute gift to the surviving spouse or cohabitee of everything else.

- *Where the other spouse or cohabitee is mentally incapable*

Another situation where a life interest trust may be appropriate is where the surviving spouse or cohabitee is or may become mentally incapable. There is little point in giving the surviving spouse an absolute interest if he or she is mentally incapable. So in these circumstances it seems that one way of providing for the surviving spouse would be to give him a life interest.

A word of warning—if the surviving spouse is in a care home already, or goes into one shortly after the death of the first spouse or cohabitee, then the local authority might try to mount a claim on behalf of the surviving spouse under the Inheritance (Provision for Family and Dependants) Act 1975 if they are funding the care home fees of the spouse.

- *Where a beneficiary is likely to become bankrupt*

Another situation where a life interest trust may be desirable is where the main beneficiary might go bankrupt. If that beneficiary is given an absolute interest, then any absolute gift will be lost if the beneficiary is made bankrupt. If the beneficiary only has a life interest, then the capital will not be lost in such a situation.

The trustees can be given power to hand out capital if that should be necessary. They can also be given power to terminate the life interest.

- *Where a beneficiary is having matrimonial difficulties*

Another situation where a life interest trust may be appropriate is where a child is having matrimonial difficulties.

An absolute gift to the child will be part of the capital as far as that child is concerned, and a divorce court may order that it should be transferred to the other spouse.

Note that the divorce court may be able to vary a life interest settlement.

DISCRETIONARY TRUST

16.2   Discretionary trusts offer flexibility, but at the same time they involve a loss of control as to the final destination of the assets.

In what circumstances can they best be used?

- *Nil rate band (NRB) discretionary trust coupled with power to accept an IOU or impose a charge.*

This is a very popular way of creating trusts. Both spouses give NRB legacies to trustees of a discretionary trust, the residue to the spouse. The trustees have power to accept an IOU from the surviving spouse for the NRB legacy, or to impose a charge.

When the surviving spouse dies, the IOU or the amount secured by the charge is deductible from his or her estate, thereby preserving the NRB of the first spouse to die, and reducing the amount of IHT payable on the death of the second spouse.

These trusts are discussed in detail in **Chapter 25** beginning at para **29**.

- *Discretionary trust to provide for disabled spouse*

In the opinion of the author, this is the most appropriate type of provision for a spouse who is mentally incapacitated, for example who suffers from Alzheimer's disease. It enables the trustees to make whatever provision they consider appropriate for the surviving spouse.

It also enables the trustees to agree a compromise of any claim on behalf of the disabled spouse under the Inheritance (Provision for Family and Dependants) Act 1975.

- *Second homes*

This scheme has been affected by changes in the Finance Act 2004.

Usually it is not possible to claim private residence exemption on the sale of a second or holiday home, but the scheme outlined here has enabled this to happen.

Parents settled the second home on discretionary trusts, and claimed hold-over or gifts relief, so that they did not have to pay CGT. After a few months the trustees permitted a child of the settlors to occupy the property. The house was then sold with the benefit of the full private residence exemption, which included the held over gain.

As a result of the Finance Act 2004, it will not be possible to claim both hold-over or gifts relief and private residence exemption. So if the parents claim hold-over or gifts relief on the transfer to the trustees, it will not be possible to claim private residence exemption when the trustees sell. If the parents do not claim hold-over or gifts relief, and pay CGT on their gain, the trustees will be able to claim private residence exemption as far as their gain is concerned.

Example

P purchased Hill Acre for £100,000.

It is now worth £180,000.

P transfers it to the trustees of a discretionary trust; the beneficiaries are his children and grandchildren.

The trustees permit one of P's children to live in the house.

The house is now worth £200,000.

If P claimed hold-over or gifts relief on the original transfer, then the trustees cannot make use of the private residence exemption.

The held over gain of £80,000 will be chargeable, plus the £20,000 increase in value since the date of the transfer.

If P had not claimed hold-over or gifts relief, then P would have paid CGT on the gain of £80,000. However, the trustees will be able to claim private residence relief in respect of the gain attributable to their period of ownership when the house is occupied by a beneficiary.

Note that hold-over or gifts relief is not available if the settlor, settlor's spouse, settlor's civil partner or infant children who are not married or in a civil partnership, are within the class of beneficiaries.

Readers are referred to para 23.48 for a further discussion of holiday homes

- *Flexible trusts to deal with non-business assets pregnant with gains*

Clients sometimes have assets which have increased in value greatly, but which they would like to give away.

If they make absolute gifts, the donor will become liable for CGT on the gain.

Hold-over relief is normally limited to business assets, but it is available for all assets on transfers to the trustees of a discretionary trust.

So if the client wants to give away an asset with a large gain, one way of doing it is to transfer the asset to the trustees of a discretionary trust, and claim hold-over relief.

If the asset is worth more than the NRB, there will of course be an IHT liability. Similarly if the client has created other discretionary trusts in the previous seven years, there may be a liability to IHT.

Note that hold-over or gifts relief is not available if the settlor, settlor's spouse, settlor's civil partner or infant children who are not married or in a civil partnership, are within the class of beneficiaries.

TRUSTS FOR BEREAVED MINORS

16.3   The main objective of these is to provide for under-age beneficiaries. Such settlements receive special treatment for inheritance tax purposes, but not for other tax purposes.

Frequently the IHT advantages of these settlements are irrelevant as the amounts transferred are small, and there is no question of any IHT liability. The CGT and income tax consequences are often far more significant, and, if tax is the only consideration, then a bare trust may have considerable advantages. The taxation of trusts for bereaved minors is discussed in **Chapter 13**. However, tax is not always the only consideration, and many clients take the view that persons may not be mature enough to deal with a relatively large sum of money at the age of eighteen, and that the age at which they become entitled absolutely should be postponed until they are older.

GIFTS TO CHILDREN

16.4 With the abolition of accumulation and maintenance settlements, some clients may be concerned about the IHT consequences of lifetime settlements on children, or lifetime settlements or settlements by will on grandchildren, nephews, nieces contingent on the beneficiaries attaining 18, 21, 25 or possibly greater ages. Frequently, the amounts transferred to trusts for the benefit of minors will be within the NRB, and so there will not be any major problem with IHT. However, what advice can we give if they wish to give more than the NRB?

If they are the parents of the children, then they can create a trust for a bereaved minor. The tax treatment of trusts for bereaved minors is discussed in **Chapter 13**.

If the contingency is attaining the age of 18, and whilst it may be necessary to pay IHT on the parents' estate on death, there will not be any further charge to IHT.

If the age contingency is up to 25, then there is a possible charge to IHT when each child satisfies the contingency, but the rate is very low—it cannot be more than 4.2 per cent.

If anyone other than parents wants to give assets to minors, or parents wish to make a lifetime settlement on their children, then it will be subject to the relevant property regime as far as IHT is concerned.

One solution for clients who wish to benefit minors who are not their children would be to give the grandchildren a life interest in their wills with power for the trustees to terminate the life interest. It would also be possible to provide that the children become absolutely entitled on attaining a specified age, e.g. 21. Such a life interest would be an immediate post death interest. IHT will be payable on the clients' estate if it is large enough. However when the life interest terminates, if the children become absolutely entitled, there will not be any IHT payable. The reason for this is that the children who are life tenants are deemed to an underlying trust assets as far as IHT is concerned, so they already own the assets. When the children become absolutely entitled, there is therefore no charge to IHT.

SUMMARY

16.5

A life interest trust may be appropriate in the following situations:

- *where the parties have children from previous relationships, and wish to ensure those children benefit;*
- *where the other spouse or cohabitee is mentally incapable;*
- *where a beneficiary is likely to become bankrupt;*
- *where a beneficiary is having matrimonial difficulties*

Discretionary trusts are appropriate:

- *NRB discretionary trust coupled with power to accept an IOU or impose a charge.*
- *Discretionary trust to provide for disabled spouse*
- *Flexible trusts to deal with non-business assets pregnant with gains.*

Trust for children:

- *Trust for a bereaved minor;*
- *Life interest trust.*

Chapter 17

Perpetuities and Accumulations

Accumulation periods and, to a lesser extent, the rule against perpetuities must not be ignored.

PERPETUITIES

17.1   The rule against perpetuities may not cause any great problems because of the 'wait and see' rule. However, the basic rule is that gifts must vest within the period of lives in being plus 21 years. Before the Perpetuities and Accumulations Act 1964, the rule was strict. If there was any possibility of the gift vesting outside that period, it was void.

Example

T's will provides 'I give £100,000 to the first grandchild of mine who becomes a solicitor'.

The gift must vest within a period of lives in being more than 21 years.

Grandchildren living at T's death, and T's children, are clearly lives in being. But it is possible that a grandchild might be born after T's death, who might qualify as a solicitor more than 21 years after the death of T's children and grandchildren living at the date of T's death. As it might vest outside the perpetuity period, the gift would have been void at common law.

However, since the Perpetuities and Accumulations Act 1964, the rules have been relaxed. The gift is not void from the outset—it will be necessary to wait and see if it vests within the perpetuity period of lives in being plus 21 years. If it does not, it is void.

It is also possible to specify a perpetuity period of years not exceeding 80 years.

ACCUMULATIONS

17.2   It is not possible to accumulate income indefinitely.

Perpetuities and Accumulations

So if there is a discretionary trust, there are limits on how long the trustees can hold on to the income and not hand it to the beneficiaries.

The permitted accumulation periods are:

- the life of the grantor or settlor;
- a term of 21 years from the death of the settlor;
- the duration of the minority or respective minorities of any person or persons living or *en ventre sa mere* at the death of the settlor;
- the duration of the minority or respective minorities of any person or persons who under the limitations of the instrument directing the accumulation would for the time being if, of full age, be entitled to the income directed to be accumulated;
- a term of 21 years from the making of the disposition;
- the duration of the minority or the respective minorities of any person or persons in being at the date of the making of the disposition.

Thus, you can accumulate for the life of the grantor or settlor, for 21 years from the death of the settlor or the date of the settlement, or for the minority of a beneficiary.

If a period chosen is in excess of that permitted by law, it is only the excess which is void. However, if the accumulation period exceeds the perpetuity period, then it is void.

Most precedents choose an accumulation period of 21 years; thereafter the income must be distributed.

PART II

Chapter 18

Overview

LIFETIME PLANNING

18.1   If the client wishes to take steps to mitigate liability for inheritance tax (IHT) during his lifetime, then the following courses of action are available:

- Make use of the lifetime exemptions from IHT.

- If the client is entitled as a remainderman under a life interest trust created before 22 March 2006 where the life tenant is treated as having an interest in possession or under an immediate post death interest, and is never likely to need the capital, make a gift of the reversionary interest. It will probably not have any IHT or capital gains tax (CGT) implications.

- If the lifetime gift is not covered by one of the lifetime exceptions from IHT, then it will be a potentially exempt transfer (PET) if it is an absolute gift or a gift to a trust for a disabled person, which will be exempt if the donor survives for seven years after making the gift. It may be possible to take out insurance to cover the possibility of death within seven years of making the gift.

- It may appear that the client has no spare assets to give away; it may be possible to create assets to give away.

- If the client has assets which qualify for agricultural property relief ('APR') or business property relief ('BPR'), these can be made the subject of a lifetime gift, and there may be a reduced or no liability for IHT.

- Assets which do not qualify for APR or BPR could be sold, and the proceeds invested in assets qualifying for APR or BPR. These assets can then be made the subject of a lifetime gift.

- It may be possible to freeze the value of assets, so that any increase in value passes to children or grandchildren without any IHT liability.

- It may be possible to enter into a scheme concerning the home which may result in a saving of IHT. The following ideas are considered in this book:

  - use of the full consideration exemption;
  - co-ownership;
  - replacement of property or a gift of cash which is used to purchase a house;
  - sale of house to a relative;
  - sale of property to a life interest trust;
  - seven-year gap between lease and gift of freehold;
  - grant of an option;
  - reversionary lease;
  - other methods of saving IHT.

All apart from the first four and the last ideas are affected by the income tax charge on pre-owned assets, and this will probably deter most clients from using them.

WILLS

18.2   Most of the ideas considered in this book involve trying to preserve the nil rate band of the first spouse to die. The ideas suggested are:

- NRB gift to the children, residue to spouse;
- Gift of a half share in the matrimonial home direct to children or trustees;
- NRB discretionary trust, residue to spouse; NRB legacy to be satisfied by appropriating the whole or part of the share of the first spouse to die in satisfaction of the legacy;
- NRB discretionary trust, residue to spouse; trustees can accept an IOU or impose a charge for the NRB legacy.

Most of the suggestions contained in this book can also be used by cohabitees.

Chapter 19

Lifetime Gifts and the Use of the Exemptions

This is very simple tax planning, but nevertheless it can save a substantial amount of IHT.

ANNUAL EXEMPTION

19.1   The annual exemption for gifts of £3,000 per annum is well known. If it is not used one year, it can be carried forward to the next tax year, but it cannot be carried forward to subsequent years. Similarly, if it is not used in full, the balance can be carried forward to the next year, but not to subsequent years.

£3,000 does not seem to be very much, but it can mount up. A wealthy client who can afford to give away £3,000 per year from the age of 40, and who lives to the age of 80, could give away £120,000. If it remained in the donor's estate, then it might have to bear inheritance tax (IHT) at 40 per cent—£48,000.

Clients of any age should be advised to make use of this exemption.

The exemption is not only available on gifts to individuals. It is also available on gifts to the trustees of a settlement.

What is the position if the client makes several gifts of £3,000 in a tax year? The annual exemption is applied in chronological order.

What is the position if the gifts are made on the same day? The annual exemption is applied pro rata.

Another scenario which might be open to challenge is if the client sells a house to a child, and leaves the purchase price outstanding. If the client releases £3,000 of the debt each year, the HMRC may invoke the associated operations rule (see para **15.6**).

SMALL GIFTS

19.2   Small gifts of £250 per person per year are exempt.

This exemption ensures that gifts at Christmas and birthdays to relatives and friends are not treated as transfers of value. It would be impracticable if they were.

It is not possible to claim both the small gifts exemption and the annual exemption in respect of gifts to the same individual, so £3,250 cannot be given to the same person each year. £250 would not be exempt.

NORMAL EXPENDITURE OUT OF INCOME

19.3   A transfer of value is an exempt transfer if, or to the extent that, it is shown that:-

(*a*)   it was made as part of the normal expenditure of the transferor;

(*b*)   (taking one year with another) it was made out of his income;

(*c*)   after allowing for all transfers of value forming part of his normal expenditure, the transferor was left with sufficient income to maintain his usual standard of living.

There is no definition of 'usual standard of living'.

'Normal expenditure' means that it must be clear from the outset that the payment is going to be regular, and that a pattern of payments is established. One payment cannot come within this exemption, although if there is evidence that it was likely to continue, but because of the donor's death he was unable to continue the payments, it is arguable that it should be treated as an exempt transfer.

This is a useful exemption applying to the whole spectrum of incomes. It clearly applies to wealthy clients. A client in receipt of an income of £1.5 million who can live on £1 million can safely give away £500,000 each year without any IHT liability.

It also applies to people on lesser incomes who can live on part of their income. A person earning £100,000 per annum who can safely live on £50,000 can give away the remainder without incurring any IHT. Similarly, a person earning £30,000 per annum who can live on £20,000 can give away the remaining £10,000 without incurring any IHT liability.

There is no definition of what is meant by normal expenditure out of income. It would therefore be necessary to produce evidence of the normal standard of living enjoyed by the donor, and that it had not been reduced by the gift or gifts, and so any client considering making use of this exemption should be advised to prepare accounts of their expenditure both before and after making use of this exemption, and also file receipts relating to their expenditure. On death, if the normal expenditure out of income exemption is claimed, it is necessary to complete a form, D3a, showing the income of the deceased, and expenditure for any year in the seven years up to death for which this exemption is claimed.

The amount of the payment can fluctuate each year. Incomes can go up and down, and if the income goes down it means that the taxpayer will have less to give away after maintaining his or her normal standard of living.

The recipient does not have to be the same person. So a grandparent with several grandchildren and spare income can benefit different grandchildren each year.

Is it possible to save up the surplus income and give it in one large lump? Assume that the taxpayer has £10,000 per year of income left after maintaining his normal standard of living. Can he save up the £10,000 for, say, five years, and then give £50,000 to a child, and claim the normal expenditure out of income exemption for this amount? It is probable that this would be regarded as a gift of capital, and not within the normal expenditure out of income exemption.

GIFTS IN CONSIDERATION OF MARRIAGE

19.4   Transfers of value made by gifts in consideration of marriage are exempt to the extent that the values transferred in respect of any one marriage (calculated as values on which no tax is chargeable) do not exceed:

(*a*)   in the case of a gift by a parent, £5,000; all four parents can give £5,000, so the total is £20,000;

(*b*)   in the case of grandparents and great-grandparents, £2,500;

(*c*)   in other cases, £1,000.

The exemption is also available if the assets are transferred to the trustees of a settlement created on marriage. So if a life tenant is getting married, £5,000 can be transferred to the trustees of the settlement by each parent.

GIFTS FOR THE MAINTENANCE OF THE FAMILY

19.5   This exemption is designed to ensure that gifts to children and other family members for their maintenance are not treated as transfers of value.

Strictly, every time a parent gives money to a child who is at university, it is a transfer of value. However, no IHT will be payable as it will usually come within this exemption.

A disposition is not a transfer of value if it is made—

(a) by one party to a marriage in favour of the other party to the marriage or a child of either party and is for the maintenance of the other party, or for the maintenance, education or training of the child for a period ending not later than the year in which he attains the age of 18 or, after attaining the age, ceases to undergo full-time education and training;

(b) in favour of a child who is not in the care of a parent of his and is for his maintenance, education or training for a period ending no later than the year in which he attains the age of 18, or, after attaining that age, ceases to undergo full-time education or training.

Gifts made to a child over 18 under this category are only exempt if before attaining that age the child has for substantial periods been in the care of the person making the disposition.

(c) in favour of a dependent relative of the person making the disposition and is a reasonable provision for his care and maintenance.
'Dependent relative' is defined as meaning in relation to any person:

   (i) a relative of his, or of his spouse, who is incapacitated by old age or infirmity from maintaining himself; or
   (ii) his mother or his spouse's mother, if she is widowed, or living apart from her husband, or a single woman in consequence of dissolution or annulment of marriage.

(d) in favour of an illegitimate child of the person making the disposition and is for the maintenance, education or training of the child for a period ending not later than the year in which he attains the age of 18 or, after attaining that age, ceases to undergo full-time education or training.

Clearly, parents can make use of this exemption, but it is more difficult for grandparents to make use of it. They can only do so in favour of a grandchild if the grandchild is not in the care of their parents, and if the grandchild is over 18 the transfer will only come within the exemption if the grandchild has been in the care of the grandparents for substantial periods of time.

Maintenance is not defined. Clearly, income payments are covered, but could a capital payment come within it? Parents frequently purchase houses for their children to live in when they are at university—it is possible that the gift of a house comes within this exemption. Even if it did not, it will have no IHT consequences if the parents survive for seven years after the gift.

SPOUSE EXEMPTION

19.6   Section 18(1) provides that a transfer of value is an exempt transfer to the extent that the value transferred is attributable to property which becomes comprised in the estate of the transferor's spouse or, so far as the value transferred is not so attributable, to the extent that the estate is increased.

This exemption is well known. Transfers between spouses are exempt, although if the transferor spouse is domiciled in the United Kingdom, and the transferee spouse is not, there is a limit of £55,000. In addition, if the deceased's NRB has not been exhausted by lifetime gifts, the deceased can give the non-UK domiciled spouse the NRB plus £55,000 without incurring any IHT liability.

If both spouses are wealthy, then the spouse exemption is not of much use in any tax saving scheme. However, if one spouse is wealthy, and the other has nothing, then the exemption may be useful to save tax. The wealthy spouse can transfer assets to the not so wealthy spouse so that that spouse can make use of the nil rate band and the lifetime exemptions from IHT.

The use of the spouse exemption is explored below at para 19.13.

ALLOCATIONS OF EXEMPTIONS

19.7   What is the position if the donor makes gifts which could qualify for several exemptions? It may be possible to claim more than one exemption on the same transfer.

Example

Assume that the donor has an income of £50,000 per year, and spends £30,000 maintaining his standard of living. He wants to give £28,000 to his daughter on the occasion of her marriage.

£20,000 would come within the normal expenditure out of income exemption, £5,000 within the marriage exemption. The remaining £3,000 would be covered by the annual exemption.

However, in order to claim the normal expenditure out of income exemption, there must generally be a series of payments, and so the donor would have to continue making the payments.

USES OF *INTER VIVOS* EXEMPTIONS

19.8   A wealthy client who has more than enough money to provide for his or her needs can save substantial amounts of IHT by making use of the lifetime exemptions. Many clients will not be wealthy enough to take advantage of these savings, but there will be some middle income clients who will want to make use of them.

NORMAL EXPENDITURE OUT OF INCOME

10-year endowment policy

19.9   If there are children or grandchildren, the client can take a 10-year endowment policy on his life and declare himself to be a trustee of the policy in favour of the children or grandchildren. The policy must last for 10 years in order to obtain favourable treatment as far as income tax is concerned.

The original declaration of trust is a PET, but it will not usually give rise to any IHT liability. For IHT purposes, the value of the policy is the higher of the market value or the premiums paid. Unless the client pays a lump sum for the policy, when a policy is first taken out the market value is usually nil. If no premiums have been paid, then the value transferred will be nil. Even if a premium has been paid, it will often be within the normal expenditure out of income exemption or annual exemption.

If the parent continues to pay the premiums, there will often be no IHT consequences because each payment will usually be within the normal expenditure out of income exemption or the annual exemption.

Policy to pay IHT

19.10   A donor who makes a PET may take out a life policy to fund the IHT which will be due if the donor dies within seven years of making the gift. The policy should be made the subject of a declaration of trust, and this will constitute a PET. Normally there will be no IHT consequences because the value of the policy is nil or very small.

If the donor continues to pay the premiums, frequently there will be no IHT consequences because of the annual exemption or the normal expenditure out of income exemption.

These policies can also be used to fund the IHT payable on the death estate. Such policies should be made the subject of a declaration of trust in favour of the beneficiary who will ultimately have to bear the IHT as otherwise it will be part of the estate of the deceased for IHT purposes.

Deed of covenant

19.11   Deeds of covenant in favour of a grandchild or adult child will also come within this exemption.

Parents or grandparents wishing to make gifts to children or grandchildren on a regular basis should consider entering into deeds of covenant in favour of the child or grandchild. Any payments under it could within the normal expenditure out of income exemption, or annual exemption.

Since 15 March 1988 these covenants have had no consequences from an income tax point of view. They are not taxable in the hands of the recipient, and the payer cannot deduct them.

Maintenance of the family

19.12   The main use of this exemption is the payment of school fees, or payments for the maintenance of children at university, but probably not if paid by grandparents. They can only do so in favour of a grandchild if the grandchild is not in the care of the parents, and if the grandchild is over eighteen, the grandchild must be in full time education or training—and then the transfer will only come within the exemption if the grandchild has been in the care of the grandparents for substantial periods of time.

Spouse exemption

19.13   The spouse exemption is not of much use in any tax planning scheme unless one spouse is wealthier than the other. If they both have assets in excess of the nil rate band, not much use can be made of it. But if one spouse is wealthier than the other, the spouse exemption can be used:

(*a*)   to enable both spouses to make full use of the NRB;

(*b*)   to enable both spouses to make full use of the lifetime exemptions and PETS;

(*c*)   to equalise estates in order to effect a saving of income tax and CGT.

Where a wealthy person is married to a spouse with nothing, the nil rate band of the spouse with nothing will be lost if that spouse dies first. However, if the wealthy spouse transfers assets to the value of the NRB to the spouse with nothing, that spouse can then give that amount to the children, and if that spouse dies first, the NRB of that spouse is not lost.

A wealthy spouse paying higher rate tax could also minimise liability for income tax or CGT by transferring assets to the spouse with nothing so that any resulting income or capital gain is taxed at lower or basic rate tax.

Be wary of the associated operations rule (see para **15.6**), although HMRC have indicated that they will not invoke this rule unless it was a condition that the second gift would be made. So if one spouse transfers assets to another spouse, there must be no understanding that the donee spouse will make gifts to the children.

Use of the nil rate band

19.14   If the gift is a PET, no IHT will be payable if the donor survives for seven years, and in any event it will not be chargeable if the PET is within the NRB.

A gift to a trust other than a trust for a disabled person within the NRB will not incur any charge to IHT, and any gain can be held over provided it is not a settlor interested trust; for a fuller discussion of settlor interested trusts, see para **15.5**.

Such gifts will, of course, be taken into account when calculating the amount of IHT payable on the death estate if the donor fails to survive for seven years after making the gift.

POTENTIALLY EXEMPT TRANSFERS

19.15   Section 3A of the IHTA 1984 provides that a potentially exempt transfer is a transfer of value which:

(*a*)   is made by an individual on or after 18 March 1986;

(*b*)   apart from this section, would be a chargeable transfer (or to the extent to which, apart from this section, it would be such a transfer); and

(*c*)   to the extent that it constitutes either a gift to another individual or a gift into an accumulation and maintenance trust or a trust for a disabled person.

Thus, gifts to individuals, to trusts with an interest in possession and to accumulation and maintenance trusts are all PETS. If the donor survives for seven years, no IHT is payable. If the donor dies within the seven years, IHT is payable.

Taper relief may operate to reduce the amount of IHT payable if the donor survives for at least three years. Taper relief is allowed as follows:

- Transfer 3–4 years before death: 80% of tax is payable.
- Transfer 4–5 years before death: 60% of tax is payable.

- Transfer 5–6 years before death: 40% of tax is payable.
- Transfer 6–7 years before death: 20% of tax is payable.

Taper relief only reduces the amount of IHT payable—it does not reduce the value for IHT purposes, and it does not affect the value for cumulation purposes.

Example

Assume that G makes a lifetime gift of £300,000.

He dies six and a half years later leaving an estate of £500,000.

Any IHT payable on the PET will be reduced by 80 per cent. However, in calculating the IHT payable on the death estate, it is the full value which has to be taken into account.

PETs have many advantages:

- The rates of IHT payable are the rates in force at the date of death, unless they have increased.
- If they have increased, then the rate payable is the rate in force at the date of the gift. IHT has not increased in recent years. It has in fact gone down due to the increase in the NRB.
- The value on which IHT is payable on a PET is the value at the date of the gift—thus the value is frozen. However, relief is available if the asset has gone down in value since the date of the gift.

Even if the donor is not likely to survive for seven years, it is still a good idea to give away assets which may increase in value because the donor will pay IHT on the value at the date of the gift. It is not possible to lose with a PET—IHT is payable on the value transferred at the date of the gift even if the subject matter of the gift has increased in value.

It may be possible to insure against the donor dying within seven years of the PET. This is discussed above at para **19.10**.

GIFTS WITH A RESERVATION OF BENEFIT

19.16 Be careful not to infringe the rules relating to gifts with a reservation of benefit as otherwise the PET will be ineffective as far as saving IHT is concerned. If the deceased has made a gift, but nevertheless still enjoys some benefit from the property the subject of the gift, a benefit will have been reserved, and the deceased will still be deemed to own the property at the date of death.

However, the gift may be effective for other tax purposes. If parents give the house in which they are living to children, and continue living there, the gift will not be effective to save IHT, but it will be effective as far as other taxes are concerned, so that when the children sell, they will not be able to claim private residence exemption for capital gains tax unless they have been in occupation.

SUMMARY

19.17

The commonly used lifetime exemptions from IHT are:

- annual exemption;
- small gifts;
- gifts in consideration of marriage;
- gifts for the maintenance of the family;
- spouse exemption.

The normal expenditure out of income exemption can be used to fund endowment policies, policies to pay IHT, and in conjunction with deeds of covenant.

The spouse exemption can be used to channel assets to a spouse lacking assets so that they can be passed to the children.

PETs can be used to transfer the NRB every seven years.

Be careful not to infringe the rules relating to gifts with a reservation of benefit.

Chapter 20

CGT and Lifetime Gifts

INTRODUCTION

20.1   **Chapter 19** considered how it is possible to make use of the *inter vivos* exemptions from IHT. However, it must not be forgotten that any lifetime gifts could give rise to a capital gains tax (CGT) liability. This issue was considered in **Chapter 9**—the most relevant aspects as far as lifetime gifts are also considered here for the convenience of readers.

For CGT purposes, any gift of an asset will be deemed to be a disposal of that asset at market value as at the date of the gift. Similarly, any disposal to connected persons will be a disposal at market value. In so far as the gain is not absorbed by the annual exemption, it will be taxed as if it formed the top part of the donor's income for income tax purposes.

Any transfers between spouses are treated as if no gain or loss had resulted. In effect, the donee spouse takes over the acquisition costs and subsequent expenditure of the donor spouse.

Example

If a spouse buys an asset for £500,000, and gives it to his or her spouse when it is worth £700,000, the donee spouse will be deemed to have acquired it for £500,000.

There are anti-avoidance provisions in s 19 of the Taxation of Chargeable Gains Act 1992 dealing with the disposal of assets in a series of transactions; for a fuller discussion of this section, please see *Tottel's Capital Gains Tax*.

TAPER RELIEF

20.2   This replaced indexation allowance, and operates by reducing the gains made in each tax year after deducting the expenditure by a certain percentage. The percentage varies depending on whether you are dealing with business assets or non-business assets. The relief is set out below.

Number of whole years in qualifying holding period	Rate of relief for business assets	Rate of relief for non-business assets
0	100	100
1	50	100
2	25	100
3	25	95
4	25	90
5	25	85
6	25	80
7	25	75
8	25	70
9	25	65
10	25	60

The relief is far more generous for business assets than non-business assets.

For business assets, relief starts after one year's ownership.

For non-business assets, it starts after three years.

Business assets are defined in Sch A1 to TCGA 1992.

HOLD-OVER OR GIFTS RELIEF

20.3   The effect of hold-over or gifts relief is to reduce the donee's acquisition cost to that of the donor plus any allowable expenditure. This relief applies to gifts. It does not provide a complete exemption from CGT—all it does is to postpone the liability until the asset is sold.

Example

Assume that F is the majority shareholder in F Ltd, a company he founded.

The shares are now worth £900,000.

He is proposing to give the shares to his children.

If both F and the children elect to claim hold-over relief, the effect will be that the CGT liability will be postponed until the children sell or dispose of the shares. Then any gain will be computed by deducting the initial cost and subsequent expenditure by F.

This relief used to mean that there was no need to worry about CGT on *inter vivos* gifts. However, the relief was restricted to a limited class of assets in 1989. It is now confined to the following assets:

(i) it is, or is an interest in, an asset used for the purposes of a trade, profession or vocation carried on by:

- the transferor, or
- his personal company, or
- member of a trading group of which the holding company is his personal company; or

(ii) it consists of shares or securities of a trading company, or of the holding company of a trading company, where:

- the shares or securities are not listed on a recognised Stock Exchange or the trading company or holding company is the transferor's personal company;

(iii) agricultural property, or an interest in agricultural property, within the meaning of Ch. II of Pt V of the Inheritance Tax Act 1984;

(iv) it is a chargeable transfer within the meaning of the Inheritance Tax Act 1984 (or would be but for s 19 of that Act) and is not a potentially exempt transfer (within the meaning of that Act);

(v) it is an exempt transfer by virtue of ss 24, 26, 27 and 30 of that Act.

'Personal company' in relation to an individual means a company the voting rights in which are exercisable as to not less than 5% by that individual.

'Holding company', 'trading company' and 'trading group' have the meanings given by para 22 of Sch A1 to TCGA 1992.

Transfers to political parties, or for the public benefit, or to maintenance funds for historic buildings and designated property, are exempt from IHT.

Both the donor and the donees or trustees must agree to claim hold-over relief.

Note that hold-over relief is also available on transfers to the trustees of a discretionary trust, whether or not business assets are transferred to the trustees. The reason for this is that IHT may be payable on the transfer, and usually the HMRC do not charge the same transaction with two taxes.

If hold-over relief is not available, consider the following points:

(a) It may be possible to pay the CGT by instalments. This can be done if the gift is of:

(i) land or an estate or interest in land;
(ii) shares or securities giving control of a company; or
(iii) unquoted shares or securities.

Interest runs from the date the tax is due (TCGA 1992, s 281).

(b) No CGT is payable on gifts of non-chargeable assets including cash.

SUMMARY

20.4

- A gift of an asset is a deemed disposal at market value.
- Taper relief may reduce the CGT payable.
- Hold-over relief may be available to postpone the date when the CGT has to be paid.
- It is possible to pay the CGT by instalments in the case of gifts of certain types of assets.

Chapter 21

Tax Treatment of Pre-owned Assets

21.1   The Finance Act 2004 imposed a charge to income tax on the equivalent of the market rent in respect of a house a person once owned but still occupies without reserving a benefit. This charge also applies to chattels which the donor has given away, and has not reserved any benefit, but is still enjoying. So if parents give away an antique, but still continue to use it without triggering the gift with reservation rules, they will be charged to income tax on a percentage of the capital value of the asset. These provisions have retrospective effect, and catch transactions entered into after 18 March 1986.

The following transactions are excluded from the charge (Finance Act 2004, Sch 15 para 10):

(*a*)   A disposal of the chargeable person's whole interest in the property, except for any right expressly reserved by him over the property, either:

   (i)   by a transaction made at arm's length with a person not connected with him, or
   (ii)   by a transaction such as might be expected to be made at arm's length between persons not connected with each other.

   If parents sell the house to children at the full market value, and this price is paid, and the parents remain in occupation, it is probable that the charge will not apply as it is the type of transaction which might be expected to be made at arm's length between persons not connected with each other.

(*b*)   The property was transferred to the spouse or civil partner of the transferor, or, where the transfer has been ordered by the court, to his former spouse.

(*c*)   A disposal by way of gift (or, where the transfer is for the benefit of his former spouse or civil partner, in accordance with a court order), by virtue of which the property became settled property in which his spouse or civil partner or former spouse or former civil partner is beneficially entitled to an interest in possession.

Transactions between spouses are not caught. So if the house is vested in the name of one spouse, and is transferred to the other spouse, the charge to income tax will not apply, even if the donor spouse is still living in the house. If one spouse transfers the matrimonial home into joint names, the charge will not apply.

(d) The disposal was a disposition falling within s 11 of the Inheritance Tax Act (IHTA) 1984 (dispositions for the maintenance of the family).

(e) The disposal is an outright gift to an individual and is for the purposes of IHTA 1984 a transfer of value that is wholly exempt by virtue of s 19 (annual exemption) or s 20 (small gifts).

Paragraph 11 of Sch 15 prescribes the exemptions from the charge.

(a) The provisions in the Schedule relating to land, chattels and intangible property do not apply where the estate of a person includes:

   (i)   the relevant property, or

   (ii) other property:

- which derives its value from the relevant property, and
- whose value, so far as attributable to the relevant property, is not substantially less than the value of the relevant property.

(b) If the property has been subject to a gift with reservation.

If a benefit has been reserved in property, then it will of course be part of the donor's estate as far as IHT is concerned, and the charge to income tax will not apply. So if parents give their house to a child, and continue living there, a benefit will have been reserved, and the house will still be part of the parent's estate on death (Finance Act 2004, Sch 15 para 11(5)(a)).

(c) The taxpayer has given a share in the house to another person, and occupies the house together with the person (Finance Act 2004, Sch 15 para 11(5)(c));

If a mother and an adult child are living in the house in the sole name of the mother, and it is transferred into joint names, there will not be any charge to income tax.

(d) Finance Act 1986 Sch 20 para b(1)(a) applies. This provides that in the case of property which was interest in land or a chattel, retention or assumption by the donor of actual occupation of the land is to be disregarded if it is for full consideration in money or money's worth.

(e) Finance Act 1986 Sch 20 para 6(1)(b) applies. This provides that in the case of an interest in land, any occupation by the donor of the whole or any part of the land shall be disregarded if:-

(i)   it results from a change in the circumstances of the donor since the time of the gift, being a change which was unforeseen at the time and was not brought about by the donor to receive the benefit of this provision; and

(ii)   it occurs at a time when the donor has become unable to maintain himself through old age, infirmity or otherwise; and

(iii)   it represents a reasonable provision by the donee for the care and maintenance of the donor; and

(iv)   the donee is a relative of the donor or his spouse (Finance Act 2004, Sch 15 para 11(5)(d)).

This provision is intended to deal with the situation where the donor makes a genuine gift of the house without reserving any benefit. The donor may become unable to maintain himself through illness or just old age. In this situation, if the donor moves back into the house, there will not be any reservation of benefit.

(*f*)   If the taxpayer is a non-resident in the United Kingdom; if the taxpayer was resident, but not domiciled, then the charge will only apply if the property is situated in the United Kingdom (Finance Act 2004, Sch 15 para 12(1) and (2)).

(*g*)   The aggregate notional annual values do not exceed £5,000.

(*h*)   The taxpayer was formerly the owner of an asset only by virtue of a will or intestacy which has subsequently been varied by agreement between the beneficiaries (Finance Act 2004, Sch 15 para 16).

So, if the taxpayer is a beneficiary under a will or intestacy, and enters into a deed of variation thereby avoiding the gift with reservation of benefit rules, the charge to income tax will not apply.

There are similar provisions dealing with situations where the taxpayer has contributed to the acquisition of any property by another person.

Taxpayers subject to the charge can elect to have the property treated as part of their estate for IHT purposes, and avoid the charge. The time limit for making the election is the 31st January following the end of the tax year in which the liability to income tax arose.

With regard to existing schemes, taxpayers may elect before 31 January 2007 to pay the income tax or to have the property concerned taxed as part of their estate for IHT purposes. The Finance Act 2007 allows late elections to be made.

Chapter 22

Lifetime Tax Planning Schemes

INTRODUCTION

22.1   A client with more than enough to provide for himself for the rest of his life should give away what he does not need. It is not easy to know how much a client will need to provide for himself for the rest of his life, but as long as the client is satisfied that he has enough, then he should start giving away his assets.

It may be that there is little scope for the middle income client at the bottom end of the scale to give away very much, but, at the top end of the scale, this may be a possibility—particularly if the client is quite elderly.

The simplest type of gift is a gift of cash. Many clients have substantial amounts of money in deposit accounts. A gift of cash is just as effective from an inheritance tax (IHT) point of view as other property. Of course, there is no liability for capital gains tax (CGT).

If the donee intends to use the money to buy an asset, it may be better for the donor to buy the asset, for example a new car, and then give it to the donee. Unless HMRC invokes the associated operations rule, and there is a risk that the rule will be invoked, the value given away will be the value of the asset at the date of the gift, not the purchase price, and with many new cars the value of the car once it has been driven away from the dealer is considerably less than the purchase price.

THE SCOPE FOR CREATING SURPLUS ASSETS

22.2   It may appear that a client has no spare assets to give away. However, it may be possible to create surplus assets.

For example, a client with investments producing a low yield may be able to invest in assets with a higher yield, thus freeing some of his assets.

Another possibility is to advise an elderly client who is living off income to live off capital as well. This should free some assets, which can then be given away. Obviously, it is necessary to ensure that the capital will not run out.

The client could also borrow money on the security of the home, making use of the various equity release schemes available. The borrowed money could then be made the subject of a gift to children or grandchildren, or used to create a settlement.

OTHER TYPES OF ASSETS SUITABLE FOR LIFETIME SCHEMES

22.3 Apart from gifts of cash, the client should consider making gifts of the following:

- life insurance policies;
- assets yielding little or no income;
- assets likely to increase in value, or whose value is temporarily depressed.

Life insurance policies

22.4 If nothing is done, the proceeds will form part of the estate of the life insured. They can be made the subject of a declaration of trust. The initial transfer is a transfer of value, and the value transferred will be the higher of the market value and the premiums paid. Thus, if the policy is made the subject of a declaration of trust when it is first taken out, it will usually have little or no value if premiums are to be paid on a regular basis—in the early days of a policy the market value will be nil, and if one premium has been paid, it will probably have no IHT consequences as it will come within one of the lifetime exemptions from IHT. If the donor continues to pay the premiums, it will usually have no IHT implications as the payments will come within the annual exemption or normal expenditure out of income exemption.

Assets yielding no or little income

22.5 The home comes under this head. Tax planning opportunities with regard to the matrimonial home are explored in **Chapter 23**.

Valuable antiques and paintings are also included under this head. However, be careful not to infringe the reservation of benefit rules. Parents cannot give an antique to children and still use it—that will be a reservation of benefit. If there is no reservation of benefit, but the parents are still using the antique, the income tax charge on pre-owned assets may apply (please refer to **Chapter 21** for fuller discussion).

If the client is a life tenant under a trust, and is treated as owning the assets in the trust, and the trust assets are not yielding much income, then the life tenant should consider surrendering the life interest to the remainderman, who will probably be a child. This would be a potentially exempt transfer (PET) of all the assets in the trust by the life tenant.

A remainderman who is never likely to need the capital from the interest in remainder under a trust where the life tenant is deemed to own the asset in the trust, should assign the interest whilst the life tenant is still living as it will usually not have any IHT or CGT consequences.

Readers are referred to **Chapter 8** for a discussion of the IHT treatment of trusts where the life tenant is deemed to own the underlying trust assets.

Assets likely to increase in value

22.6   This category includes shares in private companies and houses subject to tenancies.

For IHT purposes any increase in value is ignored because if the donor dies within seven years of making the gift, the value chargeable to IHT will be the value of the asset at the date of the gift. However, the free uplift on death for CGT purposes will be lost.

If the property the subject of the gift is eligible for business property relief (BPR) or agricultural property relief (APR) it may be better to give it by will as there is no CGT payable on death. The difficulty with this suggestion is that there is always a possibility that BPR or APR will be restricted in the future.

The availability of hold-over relief is another factor to be considered. If the assets are the subject of a lifetime gift qualify for this relief, then the gain can be held over. For a fuller discussion of hold-over or gifts relief, readers are referred to paras 9.9 and 10.1.

ASSET CONVERSION

22.7   Another possibility worth considering is asset conversion. Probably this is more appropriate for very wealthy clients, but there may still be middle income clients for whom it is appropriate.

Businessmen and farmers are in a very privileged position as far as IHT is concerned. If they own assets qualifying for 100 per cent APR or BPR it can be a complete exemption from IHT. The idea behind asset conversion is that the client sells assets not qualifying for this type of relief, and invests the proceeds in property qualifying for BPR or APR. The typical middle income client will not be able to make much use of the APR exemption, but it may be possible to make use of BPR by investing in private companies run by the client's children, or listed on AIM. There are obvious risks in this suggestion!

Another possibility is to invest in woodlands. This investment does not provide a complete exemption from IHT—it has to be paid if the woodland is sold, or the trees are felled (IHTA 1984, ss 125–130).

ASSET FREEZING

22.8　　The idea behind asset freezing is to freeze the value, so that the donee gets any increase in value free from IHT. The circumstances in which this course of action is worth considering are where the client perhaps does not have enough to make large gifts, or any gifts at all, but nevertheless wants to do something. The idea is that the settlor is able to recover the original amount, if necessary.

There are three possible ways of freezing the value of assets:

- loans;
- sale of assets;
- grants of options to purchase.

Loans

22.9　　This is a useful course of action if the client is not certain whether he can afford to give away any capital. The idea is to make a loan to a child or grandchild which is then invested. The client is entitled to repayment of the loan—that is frozen—but the hope is that the investments will produce a healthy return.

Dangers:

(*a*)　IHT is charged on the reduction in value of the parent's estate. If the child could not borrow the money on the commercial property market, then it is arguable that there has been a reduction in value of the parent's estate in that the child will not be able to repay the loan.

　　The effect of this would be that the client would be deemed to have made a PET of the amount of the loan.

(b) Again, to avoid any suggestion that the loan is a reduction in the value of the estate, and thereby liable to incur a possible charge to IHT, the loan should be repayable on demand. Otherwise, it would essentially be a gift, and would be treated as a PET.

(c) The income may be part of the income of the parent under anti-avoidance provisions in Income Tax (Trading and Other Income) Act 2005.

(d) It could be argued that this is a gift with reservation for IHT purposes.

There is a scheme promoted by insurance companies and financial advisers which makes use of this idea. A trust is created for the benefit of the settlor's children and grandchildren. The settlor then makes a loan to the trustees, and the trustees use the loan to purchase bonds. The trustees surrender 5 per cent each year—this can be done without incurring any tax liability. The trustees give this money to the settlor in repayment of the loan. On the death of the settlor, only the amount of the outstanding loan is chargeable to IHT.

Sale of assets

22.10   A parent sells the asset to a child at market value. The parent receives the value as at the date of the sale. As it is a market value transaction, there will be no IHT liability. The hope is that the asset will increase in value. The child will be entitled to this increase in value.

The sale may give rise to a charge to CGT, and there may be a liability to stamp duty or stamp duty land tax.

Options to purchase

22.11   Parents may grant an option to purchase assets at the market value at the date of the grant of the option. When the option is exercised, the grantee obtains the benefit of any increase in value free of IHT.

A parent who owns a holiday home could grant to a child an option to purchase the home at the value at the date of the option. When the option is exercised, the hope is that the property will have increased in value, and this increase will accrue to the child free of IHT.

Disadvantages:

(a) If the grant is not for full consideration, it will not be fully taken into account when valuing the property (IHTA 1984, s 163).

In the example, the child must pay the market price for the grant of the option.

If the child does not do so, and the parent dies, the HMRC will argue that the property should be valued at more than the price at which the option can be exercised.

Example

Assume that parents own a holiday home which is worth £200,000.

The parents grant a child the right to purchase the home for £200,000 in the next 21 years.

A third party would have paid £5,000 for this option, but the child pays £1,000.

When the parents die, the home is worth £300,000.

The HMRC may argue that the value of the home for IHT purposes is not £200,000, but somewhere between £200,000 and £300,000 because the child did not pay the market value of the option.

If the child had paid the market value for the grant of the option, then if the child exercises the option, the increase in value will accrue to the child free of any liability for IHT.

(b)   If the option is not exercised, this could be a transfer of value for IHT purposes; it would not be a PET. As it is not a PET, IHT will be chargeable immediately on the difference between the option price and the value of the property.

The child entitled to exercise the option will be deemed to have made a transfer of value of the difference between the option price and the value.

If, in the example above, the child fails to exercise the option, he will be deemed to have reduced his estate by £100,000.

(c)   There may be liability to CGT on the grant of the option.

The creation of the option is the creation of a new piece of property, and as it is new, the base cost will be nil. If it is granted by a parent to a child, then the grant will be deemed to be at market value for CGT purposes because parent and child are deemed to be connected persons for CGT purposes.

(d)   The option must be exercised within 21 years; the reason for that is nothing to do with tax—it is all to do with the perpetuity period. Options must be exercised within 21 years unless they are contained in a lease. The option must specify a perpetuity period not exceeding 21 years.

(*e*)   It is probable that this arrangement will be caught by the new income tax charge on pre-owned assets (for a fuller discussion, see **Chapter 21**).

STAMP DUTY/STAMP DUTY LAND TAX

22.12   Stamp duty applies to transfers of shares, but no duty is payable provided an instrument is certified as coming within Category L in the Schedule to the Stamp Duty (Exempt Instruments) Regulations 1987.

Stamp duty land tax is payable on any sale of land or gift of land which is subject to a mortgage where the donor assumes responsibility for the mortgage.

SUMMARY

22.13

- The best assets to give away are assets yielding little or no income, assets likely to increase in value, cash, and life insurance policies.
- It is possible to create assets to give away.
- Assets can be converted into assets qualifying for APR or BPR.
- It is also possible to freeze the value of assets.

Chapter 23

The Family Home and Lifetime Tax Planning

INTRODUCTION

23.1 For many people the home is their most valuable asset, and in many parts of the country its value frequently exceeds the nil rate band (NRB). In this situation there is a tendency to try to use the home in tax planning schemes. It is the view of the author that this is not a good idea. All the schemes involve tying up the house in some way, and if it becomes necessary to sell the house, it may be difficult to do so. It should therefore be remembered that in any estate planning involving the family home, the need to preserve it as a home is paramount. It may also be desirable to retain the ability to sell the house freely.

The right of survivorship does not apply to a tenancy in common, so tenants in common can leave their interests to whoever they like by will. An equitable joint tenancy can be converted into a tenancy in common by service of a notice under s 36(2) LPA 1925, or by agreement. HMRC accept that a posthumous variation is effective for the purposes of severance.

If the combined wealth of the spouses is unlikely to exceed the NRB for IHT purposes, it is immaterial whether or not the house is vested in the spouses as joint tenants or tenants in common. If their combined wealth is likely to exceed the NRB, it is desirable to vest the property in them as tenants in common from a tax planning point of view.

Most gifts of the matrimonial home will be potentially exempt transfers (PETs). However, it is very difficult to give away the matrimonial home and continue living there because of the reservation of benefit provisions in s 102 of the Finance Act 1986. Even a provision that the house can only be sold with the consent of the donor would be enough to bring these provisions into play.

If the reservation of benefit provisions do apply, the gift will be a nullity as far as inheritance tax (IHT) is concerned, but any gain may be subject to capital gains tax (CGT) in the hands of the donee. The donor will be deemed to own the property for IHT purposes, but not for any other purposes, so that the donee owns the property for CGT purposes. Thus, if the donee does not live in the house, he will not be able to claim the private residence exemption for CGT purposes on a sale.

There were various schemes which could be entered into with regard to the home in order to save IHT. Then along came the *Ingram* case in the House of Lords: *Ingram (executors of the estate of Lady Ingram, Re) v IRC [1999] STC 37*. Lady Ingram granted a lease to herself via a nominee, and then gave the freehold to her children. It was held that the gift of the freehold was effective for IHT purposes, so that on her death the freehold did not form part of her estate. No benefit had been reserved.

As a result of the *Ingram* decision, the Finance Act 1999 inserted a new section into the Finance Act 1986. Section 102A applies where an individual disposes of an interest in land by way of gift on or after 9 March 1999.

Section 102A(2) provides that at any time in the relevant period when the donor or his spouse enjoys a significant right or interest, or is party to a significant arrangement, in relation to the land:

(*a*)   the interest disposed of is referred to (in relation to the gift and the donor) as property subject to a reservation; and

(*b*)   section 102(3) and (4) shall apply.

Section 102A(3) provides that subject to subsections (4) and (5), a right, interest or arrangement in relation to land is significant for the purposes of subsection (2) if (and only if) it entitles or enables the donor to occupy all or part of the land, or to enjoy some right in relation to all or part of the land, otherwise than for full consideration in money or money's worth.

Subsection (4) provides that a right, interest or arrangement is not significant for the purposes of subsection (2) if:

(*a*)   it does not and cannot prevent the enjoyment of the land to the entire exclusion, or virtually to the entire exclusion, of the donor; or

(*b*)   it does not entitle or enable the donor to occupy all or part of the land immediately after the disposal, but would do so were it not for the interest disposed of.

Subsection (5) provides that a right or interest is not significant for the purposes of subsection (2) if it was granted or acquired before the period of seven years ending with the date of the gift.

These provisions all had the effect of nullifying the scheme in *Ingram*. The scheme would not now be effective. Lady Ingram would be held to have reserved a benefit.

Thus, if a parent grants a rent-free lease of his house to himself, and then gives the freehold to a child, the donor will be deemed to have reserved a benefit, and the house will form part of the donor's estate on death.

Another scheme involved the creation of a lifetime trust in favour of the spouse of the settlor. Later this was converted into a discretionary trust. The original transfer would be covered by the spouse exemption, and when the trust became a discretionary trust the reservation of benefit rules did not apply. This scheme was held to be effective in *IRC v Eversden [2003] STC 822*, but it will not now be effective as a result of changes introduced by s 185 of the Finance Act 2003.

However, it is still possible to use the house to save IHT. Before considering these schemes in detail, it should be remembered that there are three simple ways of saving IHT which almost certainly will not lead to any challenge by HMRC. These are:

- The parents could move to a smaller house, and make a PET of the money so released. On the other hand, it may be that the parents should retain the money as they may need it to provide for themselves.

- The parents could enter into some form of equity release scheme with a commercial provider, and give away the money so raised. Again, it may be that the parents should retain the money in case they need it.

- In limited circumstances, the parents could make use of Finance Act 1986 Sch 20 para 6(1)(b). This provides that in the case of property which is an interest in land, any occupation by the donor of the whole or any part of the land shall be disregarded if:

    (i)   it results from a change in the circumstances of the donor since the time of the gift, being a change which was unforeseen at that time and was not brought about by the donor to receive the benefit of this provision; and

    (ii)   it occurs at a time when the donor has become unable to maintain himself through old age, infirmity or otherwise; and

    (iii) it represents a reasonable provision by the donee for the care and maintenance of the donor; and

    (iv)   the donee is a relative of the donor or his spouse or civil partner.

This provision is intended to deal with the situation where the donor makes a genuine gift of the house without reserving any benefit. The donor may become unable to maintain himself through illness or just old age. In this situation, if the donor moves back into the house, there will not be any reservation of benefit. In addition, the income tax charge on pre-owned assets will not apply.

TAX TREATMENT OF PRE-OWNED ASSETS

23.2 The Finance Act 2004 contained provisions which charge income tax on the equivalent of the market rent in respect of a house that a person once owned but still occupies where there has been no reservation of benefit. This topic is discussed in more detail in **Chapter 21**, and, where relevant, is referred to in this chapter. It probably means that most of the schemes discussed will be unattractive to younger clients. Older clients may be prepared to pay the income tax having taken the view that the IHT saving outweighs the income tax charge.

POSSIBLE COURSES OF ACTION

23.3 The following courses of action can be taken *inter vivos* to mitigate IHT:

- use of the full consideration exemption;
- co-ownership;
- replacement of property given or a gift of cash which is used to purchase a house;
- sale of house to a relative;
- sale of property to a life interest trust;
- seven-year gap between lease and gift of freehold;
- grant of an option;
- reversionary lease.

Note that all the ideas apart form the first four will be affected by the charge to income tax on pre-owned assets, and so may not be attractive to clients.

The full consideration exemption

23.4 The parents give the freehold to the children; the children grant a lease to the parents.

The terms agreed must be the result of a bargain negotiated at arm's length with the parties being independently advised, and must follow the normal commercial criteria in force at the time. This means that the lease must be on the same terms as a lease between strangers. The parents must pay the market rent, and must enter into the repairing and other covenants that one would find in a lease between strangers. Both parents and children should be separately advised about the terms of the lease (see letter dated 18 May 1987 from the HMRC).

Ideally, the lease should be for as long as the parents are likely to live for. It is obviously not possible to predict how long someone will live. If too short a lease is granted, and the parents are alive when the lease expires, it is essential that the parents continue to pay rent at the market rate. Otherwise, if the lease terminates, and the parents do not pay any rent, the parents will be deemed to have reserved a benefit. On the other hand, if too long a lease is granted, and the parents die before the lease expires, the lease will be part of the death estate. As part of the parents' estate, IHT will have to be paid on it. The value will obviously depend on the length of the unexpired term. However, if the parents are paying the full market rent, then presumably its value will not be very great.

IHT consequences

23.5   The original gift would be a PET. For this scheme to be fully effective, therefore, the parents must survive for seven years. Even if they do not, the scheme may be partially effective—taper relief will reduce the amount of tax payable if the donor survives for three years, and IHT will be charged on the value of the property at the date of the gift, not the date of death, and so any increase in value will be free of IHT.

However, there should not be any problem with the rules relating to gifts with a reservation of benefit. As long as the parents are paying the full market rent, they will not have reserved any benefit in the home.

CGT consequences

23.6   Private residence exemption will apply to exempt any gain on the disposal by the donor parents. However, the donee children will probably not be able to make use of this exemption on a sale as they are not in residence.

If the children do move in after the death of both parents, and then sell, s 223(4) of the TCGA 1992 may provide some relief. Note that this subsection applies only to the situation where the parents have been in occupation, and then the children move in. In that situation, the gain has to be apportioned on a time basis between the periods when the parents were in occupation and when the children were in occupation.

The gain attributable to the period when the children are in occupation is not chargeable; the gain attributable to the period when the parents are in occupation is chargeable. This is done on a time basis, but the last 36 months are always excluded regardless of whether or not the children were in occupation.

The amount of gain chargeable for the time when the property is let to the parents is the amount by which it exceeds the lesser of the gain which is not chargeable or £40,000.

Example

Assume that the exempt gain attributable to the period of occupation by the donee child is £35,000, and that the non-exempt gain attributable to the period when the property was let to the parents is £60,000.

The chargeable gain is £60,000 − £35,000 = £25,000.

If the gain attributable to the period of occupation by the child was £45,000, then the chargeable gain is £20,000.

Income tax

23.7   Any rent paid is not deductible in computing liability for income tax, and will be subject to income tax in the hands of the children.

If the lease is for less than 50 years, any premium will be subject to income tax.

As long as the parents are paying the market rent, the income tax charge on pre-owned assets should not apply as any rent actually paid can be offset against the notional rent on which income tax has to be paid. In addition, if the transaction is of the type which would be entered into by strangers, then the income tax charge does not apply.

Non-tax disadvantage

23.8   The payment of a market rent may prove to be an insuperable problem with this type of scheme as the donor parents may not have sufficient income to support it.

Co-ownership

23.9   The idea of this scheme is that the parents become co-owners with the children of the home by executing a declaration of trust declaring that they hold the property on trust for themselves and their children, or assigning part of their interest to the children.

Example

Parents execute a declaration of trust of the matrimonial home under which the equitable interest is shared in the following proportions:

P1: 25%, P2: 25%, Child: 50%.

Inheritance tax

23.10   The declaration of trust will be a PET. Thus, to be fully effective, the parents must survive for seven years. Even if the parents do not survive for seven years, the scheme may be partially effective because of taper relief, and the fact that IHT is charged on the value as at the date of the gift.

The reservation of benefit provisions will not apply if:

(*a*)   the parents and the children occupy the land; and

(*b*)   the parents do not receive any benefit, other than a negligible one, which is provided by or at the expense of the children for some reason connected with the gift.

Thus, both the parents and the children must occupy the house. If the children do not do so, then the parents will be deemed to have reserved a benefit. So this scheme will only work if the children are still living at home.

The parents must not receive any collateral benefit. Thus the child must not bear more than a fair proportion of the running expenses of the home. If the child does bear more than a fair proportion, the reservation of benefit provisions will apply. It is difficult to define what is a fair proportion; if both parents and the child occupy the house all the time, it may be that the child should only bear one third of the running expenses, but if the child spends part of the week away from home, that may not be a fair proportion.

What is meant by the running expenses of the home? Clearly, it includes the cost of heating, lighting and repairs, but do they include the cost of the TV licence, replacing or repairing the washing machine etc? It is arguable that the child could pay all the other living expenses, and that no benefit would be reserved, but it is probably safer if the child pays a fair proportion of all the expenses in proportion to the child's share in the house. There is no problem with the donor bearing all the expenses.

If a child moves out, the parents will have to provide full consideration to prevent the application of the reservation of benefit rules. It is more than likely that young donee children may move out—they may get married, or get a job in another part of the country. If this happens, then the parents must pay a full market rent to the child. If the child has 50% of the house, then the parents must pay 50 per cent of the market rent to the child. If they do not pay the market rent, then they will be deemed to have reserved a benefit. What is the market rent of such a house, given that the parents have a right to occupy it? Presumably any third party taking a lease would not be prepared to pay 50 per cent of the full market rent, but it is difficult to be certain about what the discount would be. In view of this, it is probably best if the parents pay the appropriate proportion of the full market rent.

The scheme may work even if the property is shared in unequal proportions—would a transfer of 99 per cent of the property to a child in occupation be acceptable? In this scenario, HMRC may argue that a benefit has been reserved to the parents. The parents are, in effect, living in the house for nothing—so a benefit has been reserved. It is probably best if the property is shared in equal proportions.

When the parent dies, IHT will be payable on their interest in the house. HMRC may permit a 10–15% reduction in the value of the property for IHT purposes.

Note also that the co-owner need not be a child, although that will usually be the case.

Capital gains tax

23.11 The private residence exemption means that there will not be any CGT liability on the original gift. In addition there will not be any CGT liability if the parents and children who are all in occupation sell the house.

However, a child who is not in occupation will not be able to claim private residence exemption on his share if the house is sold. The parents will be able to claim it as long as they are still in occupation.

If the child moves out having lived in the house, then any gain will be apportioned on a straight line basis between the time when the child was in occupation plus 36 months and the time when the child was not in occupation minus 36 months, and CGT will be payable on the proportion of the gain attributable to the period when the child was not in occupation.

Income tax

23.12 Is this arrangement caught by the new provisions? If the child is still living in the house, the answer is that this new charge will not apply.

If the child moves out and the parents pay a market rent, then there will be no charge to income tax.

If the parents do not pay the market rent, then a benefit will have been reserved in the house, and again there will be no charge to income tax on the notional rent but there will be no saving of IHT.

Disadvantages

23.13 The main problem with this scheme is that there is no guarantee that a child will not try to enforce a sale of the property. However, if the child applied to the courts to enforce a sale, they would probably not succeed because under the Trusts of Land and Appointment of Trustees Act 1996 the court would have to consider the purpose for which the house was bought, which was to provide a home for the parents, and if that purpose still remained to be fulfilled, then a court would be very reluctant to enforce a sale of the house. Nevertheless, elderly parents could be subjected to great pressure to agree to a sale by a determined child who is short of money.

There is a major problem if the child becomes bankrupt, as the trustee in bankruptcy may try to enforce a sale of the property. There could also be difficulties if the child becomes involved in divorce proceedings as the half share in the house will be an asset the courts will take into account in deciding what order to make in the divorce proceedings. In addition, if the child predeceases the parents, IHT may have to be paid on the child's share in the house, and the share will pass under the child's will or the intestacy rules.

Another disadvantage is that if the child moves out of the property, the parents will have to pay a market rent to that child in order to prevent the reservation of benefit rules operating. They may not have the income to enable them to do this.

The child may also lose some of the private residence exemption for CGT purposes as far as his interest is concerned when the house is sold if the child has moved out of the house.

REPLACEMENT OF PROPERTY GIVEN OR A GIFT OF CASH

23.14   The parents give the home to the children, continue to live there until the children sell the house. The children buy another house with the proceeds, and the parents move in. Has a benefit been reserved in the second house?

Example

The parents give Greenacre to their children, but remain in occupation.

The children sell Greenacre and buy Redacre.

The parents move into Redacre.

Inheritance tax

23.15   There are tracing provisions contained in Finance Act 1986 Schedule 20. The effect of these is that the parents will be deemed to have reserved a benefit in the second home.

149

What would be the position if there was a considerable time lag between the sale of the first house, and the purchase of the second? It could be difficult for HMRC to apply the tracing provisions in this situation.

However, the tracing rules do not apply to gifts of cash, so if the parent gives cash to a child, and the child uses the cash to purchase a house, the tracing rules do not apply, and so the parent can live in the house without infringing the rules relating to gifts with a reservation of benefit. However, HMRC may argue that there was an understanding that the cash would be used to fund the purchase of the house, and that therefore the associated operations provisions apply. If they do, then the donor will be deemed to have reserved a benefit in the house, and on his death it will be deemed to form part of his estate for IHT purposes. If there was a long delay between the gift of cash and the purchase of the house, it might be difficult for HMRC to invoke the associated operations rule.

Capital gains tax

23.16   There should be no problem as far as the parents are concerned because of the private residence exemption, but the children will probably not be entitled to this.

Income tax

23.17   This scheme will be caught by the proposed charge to income tax on pre-owned assets.

The new rules include tracing provisions so that if the parents give the house to the children, the children sell it and buy another for the parents, and the gift with reservation of benefit rules do not apply, the parents will be assessed to income tax on the notional rent.

This is in accordance with the idea behind this tax if the house is not subject to IHT, but the parents are still living in it, then the charge to income tax applies.

However, if the parents gave cash to the children, and the gift was more than seven years before the children purchased the house, then the charge will not apply.

The gift of the cash would have become a successful PET, and so there is no charge to income tax if the money is used to purchase a house for the parents to live in.

Clients retiring abroad

23.18   It may be that clients retiring abroad will be able to make use of these ideas.

Many people who retire abroad will return to this country ultimately, or the survivor will. So parents could sell the house in this country and give the proceeds to the children, who mix the money up with theirs. The parents come back after at least seven years, and the children buy a house for the parents. It could be very difficult for HMRC to invoke associated operations rule, and there should be no problem with the new income tax charge.

However, this is only possible if the clients do not need the proceeds of sale to fund their lifestyle in France or Spain or wherever the retirement home is situated.

Another possibility is to make use of FA 1986 Sch 20 para 6(1)(b). This provides that in the case of land, any occupation by the donor of the whole or any part of the land shall be disregarded if

(i)   it results from a change in the circumstances of the donor since the time of the gift, being a change which was unforeseen at the time and was not brought about by a donor to receive the benefit of this provision; and

(ii)   it occurs at a time when the donor has become unable to maintain himself through old age, infirmity or otherwise; and

(iii)   the donee is a relative of the donor or his spouse.

This provision is intended to deal with the situation where the donor makes a genuine gift of the house without reserving any benefit. The donor may become unable to maintain himself through illness or just old age. In this situation, if the donor moves back into the house, there will not be any reservation of benefit, or any charge to income tax.

SALE OF A HOUSE TO A RELATIVE

23.19   The idea behind this scheme is to avoid the rules relating to reservation of benefit by selling the house to the children at full market value, who then grant a lease to the parents. Any increase in value then accrues to the children free of any inheritance tax liability.

Obviously the length of the lease needs careful consideration. A lease for life could be granted, and as long as it was granted for full consideration, it would not be treated as a settlement under s 43(3) of the IHTA 1984.

How do the children fund the purchase price? It is possible that they will have to borrow the purchase price. The parents could perhaps invest the sum, and use it to pay the rent. Even if they place it on deposit with a bank or building society, and the interest payable is not very much, it will help with the payment of the rent.

Another possibility is for the purchase price to be left outstanding as a loan repayable on demand. The parents could then release £3,000 of the loan each year taking advantage of the annual exemption, but there is a possibility that HMRC might invoke the associated operations rule if this is done.

Note that if the purchase price is not paid in full, this type of arrangement will probably be caught by the new charge to income tax on pre-owned assets.

Inheritance tax

23.20   No IHT should be payable on the sale as it is a commercial bargain.

If the purchase price was left outstanding as a loan repayable on demand, then it may be possible to write off £3,000 of the loan each year by making use of the annual exemption. However, as mentioned above, there are dangers in this approach in that HMRC might invoke the associated operations rule. In addition, the new charge to income tax on pre-owned assets may apply.

Capital gains tax

23.21   There should be no liability to CGT on the original sale because of the private residence exemption. However, any gain made by the children on a sale will not be covered by the exemption.

Income tax

23.22   Any rent paid will be subject to income tax in the hands of the beneficiaries, and of course the parents will not be able to deduct it in calculating their liability.

The new charge to income tax in respect of pre-owned assets does not apply if it was a disposal of the chargeable person's whole interest in the property, except for any right expressly reserved by him over the property, either:

(i)   by a transaction made at arm's length with a person not connected with him, or

(ii)   by a transaction such as might be expected to be made at arm's length between persons not connected with each other.

It is arguable that this type of arrangement will not be caught by the new charge to income tax on pre-owned assets if the purchase price is paid in full as it is 'a transaction such as might be expected to be made at arm's length between persons not connected with each other'.

If the purchase price is left outstanding as a loan due to the parents, it is probable that the charge will apply because it is not 'a transaction such as might be expected to be made at arm's length between persons not connected with each other'.

Note that the remaining ideas will be caught by the new income tax charge on pre-owned assets.

SALE OF PROPERTY TO A LIFE INTEREST TRUST

23.23   The idea of this scheme was to sell the house to trustees. No IHT was payable if this transaction was at market value. The vendors were the life tenants under the trust, and continued to reside in the property.

Example

P1 and P2 establish a trust under which they are the life tenants.

P1 and P2 sell the house to the trustees.

The purchase price is left outstanding, and is assigned to another trust.

P1 and P2 must not be beneficiaries of that trust.

Inheritance tax

23.24   The law stated here is what would have been the position prior to 22 March 2006.

There was no IHT on the original sale because the transaction was at arm's length, but if the parents assigned the right to receive the purchase money to an accumulation and maintenance settlement for the benefit of children and grandchildren that was a PET of the money given away. If it was assigned to the trustees of a life interest trust, again that was a PET of the money given away.

On the death of the first parent, his or her share under the life interest passed to the surviving spouse, and was covered by the spouse exemption, but when the surviving life tenant died, the trustees had to pay IHT on the value of the house at the date of death, less the outstanding purchase price. In effect, IHT was only payable on the increase in value.

Capital gains tax

23.25   No CGT was payable on the original sale, or on any sale by the trustees because of the private residence exemption which could still be claimed if the life tenant was in occupation. If the life tenant died, again there was no liability because of the free uplift to market value on death.

There could also be a liability to CGT on the repayment of the loan as repayment was not being made to the original creditor. Various schemes have been devised to deal with this problem.

Income tax

23.26   As from 2005, the parents will have to pay income tax on the notional market rent.

Clients who had entered into these arrangements had an option. They could elect to pay the income tax, or alternatively to have the asset treated as part of their estates for IHT purposes. The election had to be made before 31 January 2007. The Finance Act 2007 contains provisions allowing for late elections.

Stamp duty land tax

23.27   Stamp duty land tax was be payable on the sale.

Possible problems

23.28   This scheme was heavily promoted by some firms of solicitors. However, there are considerable problems associated with it; for a full discussion, please see an article in *Private Client Business* [2002] Nov/Dec at page 344 by Simon McKie. The author has attempted to summarise the points made in the article in the following paragraphs.

- The reservation of benefit rules may apply if the sale is not for full consideration.

- It may be that the outstanding purchase price should bear interest at a commercial rate, or the amount repayable should be calculated according to a formula, for example linked to the Retail Prices Index.

If it does not, then when the debt is assigned to the trust the value transferred will be discounted because of the lack of any entitlement to interest.

If the debt does not bear interest at a commercial rate, or is not linked to the RPI, then in effect there is a gift element to the transaction, and that may be sufficient to trigger the reservation of benefit rules.

- It is possible that the debt is not deductible in any event.
- The parents' estate immediately after the transfer will consist of the house plus the right to receive the outstanding purchase price.

  If the outstanding purchase price cannot be deducted in calculating the value of the house, the effect of the scheme will be to increase the size of the parents' estate.

- Assuming that the debt is deductible, then the value will vary according to whether the loan is repayable on demand, or on the death of the parents.

  If the loan is repayable on demand, then its value will be somewhere near the amount outstanding.

  If it is only repayable on the death of the parents, then its value will be discounted.

- It is possible that the settlement of the debt will invoke the reservation of benefit rules.

  It could be argued that if the debt is not repayable until the death of the parents, the trustees receive no benefit, and therefore a benefit has been reserved to the parents.

  It is possible that HMRC might invoke the associated operations rule so as to invoke the reservation of benefit rules.

- There is a possibility that the debt may not be deductible because of the rules concerning the deductibility of artificial debts.
- There may also be a tax liability when the debt is repaid as the trustees will be deemed to have acquired the debt at a discounted value; the amount of the discount will depend on whether the debt is immediately repayable.

SEVEN-YEAR GAP

23.29   This is specifically permitted by the FA 1999, and will not result in any reservation of benefit.

Example

The parents grant a lease to themselves in 2004.

They wait until 2012.

Then they give the freehold to a child or children.

Note that it may not be possible for parents to grant a lease to themselves. The parents could grant a lease to one, or alternatively it could be achieved by the use of a nominee (see *Ingram (executors of the estate of Lady Ingram, Re) v IRC [1999] STC 37*).

Inheritance tax

23.30   The gift of the freehold will be a PET. As a PET, it will only be fully effective if the donor survives for seven years after the gift. If the donor does not so survive, the gift may still be effective to save considerable amounts of tax because, if it is a PET, taper relief will apply and the value chargeable is the value at the date of the gift.

The disadvantage of this scheme is that it takes 14 years for the full benefit to be achieved.

Capital gains tax

23.31   It should be possible for the parents to claim private residence exemption.

Income tax

23.32   It is probable that the rules imposing a charge to income tax on pre-owned assets will apply. This arrangement does not appear to come within any of the exclusions or exemptions.

GRANT OF AN OPTION

23.33   The idea of this scheme is that the parent grants an option to the child to purchase the house for the market value. The hope is that the house will increase in value, and that the child will obtain the benefit of any increase in value free of IHT.

Inheritance tax

23.34   The initial grant of the option should not have any adverse IHT consequences if it is a market value transaction. When the option is exercised, the grantee should obtain the benefit of any increase in value free of IHT.

If the grant of the option is not for full valuable consideration, it may be that it will not be fully taken into account when valuing the property, and it may be that HMRC will argue that a benefit has been reserved.

Disadvantages

23.35

(*a*) As mentioned above, if the grant is not for full consideration, it will not be fully taken into account when valuing the property (IHTA 1984, s 163).

Example

Assume that the house is worth £200,000.

The parent grants a child the right to purchase the home for £200,000 in the next 21 years.

A third party would have paid £5,000 for this option.

The child pays £1,000.

The parent dies. The home is now worth £300,000.

HMRC will argue that the value of the home for IHT purposes is not £200,000 because the child did not pay the market value of the option, but somewhere between £200,000 and £300,000. It is also possible that HMRC might argue that a benefit had been reserved to the parent if the full market value for the option is not paid. If the child had paid the full market value for the grant of the option, then these problems should not arise.

(*b*) There may be liability to CGT on the grant of the option.

The creation of the option is the creation of a new piece of property, and, because it is new, the base cost will be nil. If it is granted by a parent to a child, the grant will be deemed to be at market value for CGT purposes in any event as parent and child are deemed to be connected as far as CGT is concerned. This means that the parents could incur a large liability to CGT depending on the market value of the option, which presumably depends on what will happen to house prices. However, whilst this may be a problem if the option is granted in respect of a second or holiday home, if it is the parent's principal private residence, it is probable that the grant of the option will come within this exemption.

(*c*) The option must be exercised within 21 years.

The reason for this is nothing to do with tax—it is all to do with the perpetuity period. Options must be exercised within 21 years if they are not contained in a lease. The option should specifically state that it must be exercised within 21 years or such lesser period as may be appropriate.

(*d*)   If the option is not exercised, this could be a transfer of value for IHT purposes; it would not be a PET. As it is not a PET, IHT will be chargeable immediately on the difference between the option price and the value of the property.

If in the example the child fails to exercise the option, his estate will be reduced in value by £100,000. This will be immediately chargeable to IHT, although if the child has not made other chargeable lifetime gifts, presumably no IHT will be chargeable as the transfer of value is within the NRB.

Capital gains tax

23.36   This could result in a substantial liability to CGT if the grantee of the option, the child, does not occupy the property as his only or main residence after exercising the option. If the child then sells the house, the child will not be able to claim private residence exemption.

Income tax

23.37   It is probable that the new income tax charge on pre-owned assets will apply. It could be argued that it is an excluded transaction, being 'a transaction such as might be expected to be made at arm's length between persons not connected with each other'. On the other hand, the contrary could also be argued.

REVERSIONARY LEASES

23.38   Note that HMRC may challenge this scheme.

The idea behind this scheme is to grant a lease of the home which does not come into effect until some time in the future.

Example

The parents grant a lease to their children to come into effect in 2024.

The lease is for 200 years at a peppercorn rent.

The lease must begin within 21 years because it is not possible to have a lease which comes into effect more than 21 years after it is granted. Alternatively, it could be expressed to come into effect either on the death of the surviving parent, or the expiry of 21 years, whichever is earlier.

Inheritance tax

23.39   The grant of the lease is a PET. Therefore, as long as the donor survives for seven years after the granting of the lease, there will not be any IHT implications. If the donor does not survive for seven years, then IHT will be payable on the reduction in value of the donor's estate—the difference between the value of the property not subject to the lease, and the value of the property subject to the reversionary lease. This is not necessarily disastrous because, if the donor has survived for three years, it will be possible to claim taper relief.

The great advantage of this scheme is that when the donor dies, the house will be subject to the reversionary lease, and because of that, the value will be substantially reduced.

However, one major disadvantage is what happens if one or both parents is still alive at the end of the 21-year period. In that situation, the lease will come into operation, and the parents will have to pay a market rent for their use and occupation of the house. If they do not, then the parents will be deemed to have reserved a benefit.

Note also that the parents must have acquired the house seven years before the grant of the lease, or to have acquired their interest for full consideration.

Capital gains tax

23.40   As far as the parents are concerned, CGT is not payable. The initial grant of the lease will be a deemed disposal at market value, but it should be covered by the private residence exemption.

However, when the child sells, the child will not be able to claim the private residence exemption for CGT purposes if he has not been in occupation of the house.

Income tax

23.41   This arrangement may not be caught by the new charge on pre-owned assets. The new charge catches arrangements where a person has managed to avoid the gift with reservation of benefit rules. Here there has not been any avoidance of the gift with reservation of benefit rules.

Instead the value of the house has been reduced because of the grant of the reversionary lease.

As already mentioned, HMRC may not accept that this idea works.

STAMP DUTY LAND TAX

23.42   Stamp duty land tax is not payable on a gift, unless the house is subject to a mortgage, and the donee assumes responsibility for the mortgage, when it will be.

INSOLVENCY

23.43   Do not forget the provisions in the Insolvency Act 1986 for setting aside gifts if the donor is made bankrupt.

ATTITUDE OF LOCAL AUTHORITIES/BENEFITS AGENCY

23.44   If the donor has to go into a care home, a local authority may look very carefully at any dealings with the house.

If there is a claim for a means-tested benefit, the Benefits Agency may also look very carefully at dealings with the house. If the donor has given the house to the children with the intention of assisting with a claim for benefit, then the local authority or the Benefits Agency can assess the donor as if the donor still owned the house.

Many clients are concerned about the possibility of the house being sold, and the proceeds evaporating as they are used to pay care home fees. It is worth noting that it is only a very small percentage of the population who have to go into care homes.

THE SECOND HOME

23.45   Many clients will own second or holiday homes. If parents give these to children, can the parents still stay there?

Inheritance tax

23.46   A gift of the second home to a child will, of course, be a PET.

IRInt 1001 provides some guidance as to when the rules relating to gifts with a reservation of benefit will not come into play on the gift of a second home:

> 'Some examples of situations in which we consider that FA 1986 s 102 (1)(b) permits limited benefit to the donor without bringing the GWR provisions into play are given below to illustrate how we apply the de minimis test:
>
> - a house which becomes the donee's residence but where the donor subsequently stays, in the absence of the donee, for not more than two weeks each year, or
>
> - stays with the donee for less than one month each year;
>
> - social visits, excluding overnight stays made by a donor as a guest of the donee, to a house which he had given away. The extent of the social visits should be no greater than the visits which the donor might be expected to make to the donee's house in the absence of any gift by the donor;
>
> - temporary stay for some short term purpose in a house the donor had previously given away, for example:
>
>   — while the donor convalesces after medical treatment,
>   — while the donor looks after a donee convalescing after medical treatment,
>   — while the donor's own home is being redecorated;
>
> - visits to the house for domestic reasons, for example baby sitting by the donor for the donee's children.'

Readers are referred to the full text of IRInt 1001 for examples of when the gift with reservation of benefit rules will be triggered.

Capital gains tax

23.47   Private residence exemption will not apply on any gift of a house which is not the principal private residence of the donor or donors. If the client genuinely has two homes, the client can elect which one is to be treated as the principal private residence for the purpose of this relief. If the client does not do so, HMRC will choose.

Note that this is only possible if the second home has been actually used as a residence, and it can only be backdated for two years.

Capital gains tax mitigation

23.48   Usually it will not be possible to claim private residence exemption on the sale of a second home. This next scheme has been used to mitigate CGT, but will not now work.

The parents settled the second home on discretionary trusts. This would be a deemed disposal by the parents at market value as far as CGT is concerned, but hold-over relief could be claimed on this transaction.

After a few months the trustees permitted a child of the settlors to occupy the property. The house would then be sold with the benefit of the full private residence exemption.

This scheme will not now work. There is now an option—either to claim hold-over relief or private residence exemption, but not both. So if the parents claim hold-over relief on the transfer to trustees, if the trustees sell it will not be possible to claim private residence exemption. If the parents do not claim hold-over relief, and pay CGT on their gain, the trustees will be able to claim private residence exemption as far as their gain is concerned.

Example

P purchased Hill Acre for £100,000.

It is now worth £180,000.

P transfers it to trustees of a discretionary trust; the beneficiaries are his children and grandchildren.

The trustees permit a child to live in the house.

The house is now worth £200,000.

If P claimed hold-over relief on the original transfer, then the trustees cannot make use of the private residence exemption. This means that the held-over gain of £80,000 is chargeable plus the £20,000 increase in value since the date of the transfer.

If P had not claimed hold-over relief, then when the trustees sell they will be able to claim private residence exemption.

Note that it may be that a holiday home may be a business asset for the purpose of hold-over relief. It will be if it has been avilable for letting with new to profit for at least 140 days in a twelve month period and has been let for at least 70 such days. the furnished holiday home may also qualify for business property relief as far as IHT is concerned. This will act be the case if it is an investment property managed by agents, but if the owners have been managing the property themselves, it is at least arguable that it has become a business and qualifies for business property relief.

SUMMARY

23.49   Beware of the income tax treatment of pre-owned assets.

The following courses of action can be taken *inter vivos* to mitigate IHT:

- use of the full consideration exemption;
- co-ownership;
- replacement of property given or a gift of cash which is used to purchase a house;
- sale of house to a relative.

Chapter 24

Life Assurance

24.1   Practitioners may encounter various schemes. The schemes considered in this section are not exhaustive of the schemes which may be met in practice.

TEN-YEAR ENDOWMENT POLICY

24.2   If there are children or grandchildren, the client can take a 10-year endowment policy on his life and declare himself to be a trustee of the policy in favour of the children or grandchildren. The policy must last for 10 years in order to obtain favourable treatment as far as income tax and capital gains tax (CGT) are concerned.

The original declaration of trust is a potentially exempt transfer (PET), or chargeable transfer but it will not usually give rise to any Inheritance tax (IHT) liability. For IHT purposes, the value of the policy is the higher of the market value or the premiums paid. Unless a lump sum is paid for a policy when the policy is first taken out, the market value is usually nil. If no premiums have been paid, then the value transferred will be nil. Even if a premium has been paid, it will often be within the normal expenditure out of income exemption or annual exemption.

If the parent continues to pay the premiums, frequently there will be no IHT consequences because each payment will usually be within the normal expenditure out of income exemption or the annual exemption.

POLICY TO PAY INHERITANCE TAX

24.3   A donor who makes a PET may take out a life policy to fund the IHT which will be due if the donor dies within seven years of making the gift. The policy should be made the subject of a declaration of trust, and this will constitute a PET. Normally there will be no IHT consequences because the value of the policy is nil or very small.

If the donor continues to pay the premiums, there will generally be no IHT consequences because of the annual exemption or the normal expenditure out of income exemption.

These policies can also be used to fund the IHT payable on the death estate. Such policies should be made the subject of a declaration of trust in favour of the beneficiary who will ultimately have to bear the IHT as otherwise it will be part of the estate of the deceased for IHT purposes.

If a policy is taken out to fund IHT payable on death, the trusts should reflect the interest of the beneficiaries under the will. If the beneficiaries are likely to change, a discretionary trust may be desirable, although if the trust is likely to last for more than 10 years, there may be a charge to IHT.

LOAN TO TRUSTEES

24.4   The settlor creates a discretionary trust for the benefit of his children and grandchildren. The settlor then makes a loan to the trustees, and the trustees use the loan to purchase a bond. The trustees surrender 5 per cent each year—this can be done without incurring any tax liability. The trustees give this money to the settlor in repayment of the loan. On the death of the settlor only the amount of the outstanding loan is chargeable to IHT.

Even though the settlor is not within the class of beneficiaries, it is arguable that there has been a reservation of benefit if the trustees repay the loan. This can be alleviated by someone other than the settlor creating the original settlement, and transferring a nominal amount to the trust. The real settlor then makes the loan to the trustees.

DISCOUNTED GIFT TRUST

24.5   The settlor invests in a bond, which is made subject to a trust under which the settlor is entitled to income, but the remainder is held in trust for named beneficiaries. The actuarial value of the right to receive the income is calculated, and the balance of the original premium is subject to the trust for the named beneficiaries.

The settlor is deemed to have made a disposal for inheritance tax purposes of the difference between the actuarial value of the right to receive the income and the cost of the bond. Prior to 22 March 2006, the transfer would have been a PET. However, since 22 March 2006, the inheritance tax consequences depend on the type of trust. It may be that it is an absolute trust—there are beneficiaries who are absolutely entitled. Usually these beneficiaries will be other family members. If it is an absolute trust, then the settlor will be deemed to have made a PET the actuarial value of the right to receive the income and the cost of the bond. As long as the settlor lives for seven years after the creation of the trust, no IHT will be payable on the balance of the fund. If the settlor dies within seven years, IHT will be payable. If the settlor dies after three years, IHT will be payable, but taper relief will reduce the amount of IHT payable.

Alternatively the trust may take the form of a discretionary trust. If it is a discretionary trust, then it will be a chargeable disposal for inheritance tax purposes. If the difference between the actuarial value of the right to receive the income and the cost of the bond exceeds the nil rate band for inheritance tax purposes, then inheritance tax at 20 per cent will be payable on the excess.

Of course if the difference between and the actuarial value of the right to receive the income and the cost of the bond is less than the nil rate band for inheritance tax, then none will be payable.

Whether or not any inheritance tax is payable on the difference, it is a lifetime gift, and may affect the amount of inheritance tax payable of the settlor.

Example

S purchases a bond for £500,000.

S transfers the bond to the trustees of a settlement.

S has a right to the income for life.

The actuarial value of the right to receive the income is calculated—assume it is £100,000.

There is a disposal for IHT purposes of the difference between the value of the bond and the actuarial value of the right to receive the income.

REVERTER TO SETTLOR

24.6   This scheme will not now work.

It made use of the reverter to settlor exemption for IHT purposes under which, if assets reverted to the original settlor, no IHT was payable.

The settlor took out a series of endowment policies maturing in successive years. These were placed in a flexible interest in possession trust for the benefit of children or grandchildren, but if the settlor was alive when a policy matured, it reverted to the settlor.

The original settlement was a PET for IHT purposes, but no IHT was payable if a policy matured and the proceeds reverted to the settlor. On the death of the settlor, other beneficiaries were entitled, but as long as seven years had elapsed from the original settlement, no IHT was payable.

BOND FUNDING PREMIUMS

24.7   This idea again involves the use of a bond, and surrendering 5% each year.

The bond is made the subject of a trust. Prior to 22 March 2006, that would have been a PET. After 22 March 2006 it may be a chargeable disposal for inheritance tax purposes.

However as long as the value of the bond is within the nil rate band, no inheritance tax will be payable, although the trust may affect the inheritance tax payable on the estate of the settlor if the settlor dies within seven years of the creation of the trust.

The trustees surrender 5 per cent of the bond each year, and use that to invest in a life policy on the life of the settlor for the benefit of children and grandchildren. On the death of the settlor, that policy will be free of IHT, and will pass to the beneficiaries under the trust without any IHT liability.

Example

S invests £500,000 in a bond.

The bond is made the subject of a declaration of trust.

The trustees surrender 5 per cent of the bond each year.

That 5 per cent is used to purchase a life policy for the benefit of children/grandchildren.

SPECIAL BYPASS TRUST

24.8   An employee creates a discretionary trust, possibly an offshore trust. The class of beneficiaries includes the surviving spouse. The trustees of the employee's pension scheme are requested to pay any discretionary lump sum to the trustees of the discretionary trust. The trustees can use it for the benefit of the surviving spouse if necessary, but if not, it will not form part of the surviving spouse's estate for IHT purposes.

'BACK TO BACK' POLICIES

24.9   A client may wish to increase his income, but at the same time preserve his capital.

One way of doing this is for the client to take out an annuity, and a whole life policy, and use part of the annuity to pay the premiums on the policy. This arrangement will be caught by anti-avoidance rules, unless the policy was issued on full medical evidence, and it would have been issued on the same terms if the same annuity had not been bought (SP E4). Thus if the life policy would not have been issued because of the poor health of the life assured, but is only issued because it is linked to an annuity, anti-avoidance rules will apply.

INCOME TAX CHARGE ON PRE-OWNED ASSETS

24.10   It is possible that the schemes discussed in this chapter may be subject to the new income tax charge on pre-owned assets.

(The author is indebted to Mr. Terry Arch and Mr. Mike Duncan of Eastgate Financial Services, Shepshed, for their help in compiling this chapter.)

Chapter 25

Tax-efficient Will Drafting

INTRODUCTION

25.1 The problem is how to preserve the nil rate band (NRB) of the first spouse to die.

Example

In his will H leaves everything to W.

H dies.

In her will W leaves everything to the children.

W dies.

If both spouses give everything to each other, and H dies first, all his property goes to W, and no Inheritance tax (IHT) will be payable because of the spouse exemption. When W dies, all her property and that inherited from her husband goes to the children. W's NRB is available, but the husband's has been lost.

It is possible to preserve the NRB of the first spouse to die. The possibilities considered in this chapter are:

- A nil rate band (NRB) gift to the children, residue to spouse.
- Gift of half share direct to children or trustees.
- NRB discretionary trust.
- A NRB discretionary trust, the residue to spouse; the trustees can accept an IOU for the NRB legacy or impose a charge.

NIL RATE BAND GIFT TO CHILDREN, RESIDUE TO SPOUSE

25.2   This is a simple but effective method of preserving the NRB of the first spouse to die.

Example

H gives a NRB legacy to his children, residue to W.

H dies.

No IHT is payable because of the NRB and the spouse exemption.

W leaves all her assets to the children.

W dies.

IHT is payable on W's estate in so far as it exceeds the NRB.

Both spouses give legacies up to the NRB to the children, residue to the spouse. Whichever spouse dies first, the NRB of that spouse is not lost as it would be if everything had gone direct to the spouse.

Note the following points:

(*a*)   Lifetime gifts and lifetime transfers to settlements seven years up to the date of death will reduce the amount of NRB left to give by will.

(*b*)   Be careful not to exceed the NRB as grossing up may apply. If the legacy to the children is free of tax, as the residue is going to an exempt beneficiary, the spouse, the legacy will have to be grossed up. If the legacy is subject to tax, then it will not have to be grossed up. If nothing is said in the will, then the legacy will be free of tax.

If the legacy does have to be grossed up, it will be necessary to find the amount which, after deducting IHT, will produce the actual legacy.

Example

Assume NRB is £300,000.

T leaves a will giving a legacy of £350,000 to his daughter, residue to spouse.

The legacy will have to be grossed up.

The first £300,000 will be within the NRB assuming that it has not been absorbed by lifetime gifts, leaving £50,000 chargeable to IHT.

$$£50,000 \times \frac{100}{60} = £83,333$$

The IHT of £33,333 attributable to the legacy will be borne by the residuary estate.

Practitioners will find that most precedents are drafted to take account of lifetime gifts.

(c) It may be that a limit should be imposed on the amount of the legacy.

It is necessary to ensure that the surviving spouse is left with enough to live on. The NRB usually increases each year at more than the rate of inflation. It is possible that there might be a bigger increase, which could mean that the residue is insufficient to provide for the surviving spouse.

Alternatively, it may be that the testator has enough assets to make this type of will when the will is actually made. However, the situation may be very different when the testator dies. The will should be kept under review as circumstances change, and it may be that what was reasonable provision for a spouse when the will was made will not be adequate when the testator dies in ten or twenty years' time.

(d) Be careful also to ensure that a NRB legacy does not include agricultural property and business property qualifying for 100 per cent relief as it is a waste of the relief as far as tax planning is concerned. As far as tax planning is concerned, the ideal course of action is to have a separate gift of assets which qualify for agricultural property relief or business property relief.

If the deceased leaves property qualifying for either agricultural property relief or business property relief, and he leaves this type of will, it may be that the value of that property will be attributed to both the nil rate band legacy and the residue. It should therefore be made clear in these wills whether assets qualifying for 100% APR or BPR are included or excluded.

The main problem with this scheme is that the great majority of clients do not have enough spare capital to give a NRB legacy to the children, and at the same time provide adequately for the surviving spouse. However, some clients may be able to give lesser amounts.

Is there any way that the legacy can be satisfied by a charge on the house or IOU?

The children would have to agree that they will accept a charge on the house, or an IOU from the surviving spouse for the amount of the NRB legacy, and they would only be able to agree to this if they were mentally capable adults. If they are minors or mentally incapable, they will not be able to agree. One way round this would be to give the executors power to impose charges on property, or to take an IOU in satisfaction of the legacy. On the death of the surviving spouse, the charge or IOU would be a debt due from the estate of the surviving spouse.

There are two possible problems with this suggestion—the anti-avoidance rules concerned with artificial debts, and the associated operations rules. It is the view of the author that such a suggestion may be caught by s 103 of the Finance Act 1986. There is also the possibility of a challenge on the basis of associated operations, but it is difficult to see how this arrangement could be challenged if there is an absolute gift to the children with no strings attached.

Stamp duty land tax

25.3   It is probable that stamp duty land tax will be payable if the children agree to accept an IOU or charge from the surviving spouse.

Use of the home

25.4   If one spouse owns the house absolutely, and has substantial other assets, that spouse can give a NRB legacy to the children, and the house can then be included in the residuary gift.

If the spouses are tenants in common of the house, then if they have enough assets they can give a NRB legacy to the children and the interest of each spouse in the house can be included in the residuary gift to the survivor.

Of course, the problem with this suggestion is that usually there are not enough assets in the estate to give a NRB legacy to the children, and at the same time provide adequately for the surviving spouse.

GIFT OF HALF SHARE DIRECT TO CHILDREN OR TRUSTEES

25.5   Spouses who are tenants in common can give their interests direct to the children. The surviving spouse will be entitled to occupy the property because of his or her interest. The consent of the surviving spouse to any sale should not be required, and in addition the surviving spouse must not be given any right to remain in occupation of the house. This is a simple idea and probably effective as far as saving IHT is concerned. The deceased's interest as tenant in common will not form part of the estate of the surviving spouse, and so no IHT will be payable. So if H makes a will leaving half share direct to children, and dies, when W dies his half share should not be part of her estate for IHT purposes.

In the past any requirement that the surviving spouse should have to agree to any sale has been fatal to this idea. In addition, any provision giving the surviving spouse the right to remain in occupation would also have been fatal to this idea. HMRC would say that the surviving spouse has an interest in possession in the house. Now there is a risk that HMRC will argue that the surviving spouse has an immediate post death interest, and therefore the house will be part of the surviving spouse's estate for IHT purposes if the surviving spouse has to agree to the sale or is given the right to live there.

What is the value of the half for IHT purposes? Is it one half of the market value, or does it have to be discounted because the surviving spouse has the right to remain in the house? The answer according to the next case is yes. In Personal representatives of Bernard Everall Williams deceased (SpC 392), CIR v. Arkwright Mr. and Mrs. Williams owned Ash Lane Farm as tenants in common. Mr. W left his half share to his wife in his will, and within two years of his death, Mrs. W and her daughters, the personal representatives, varied the will so as to give one half to the daughters. The question at issue was how the half share was to be valued. Was the value one half of the full vacant possession value, or did that have to be discounted because the surviving spouse had rights to remain in the house? HMRC accepted that the surviving spouse did have rights of occupation in the house.

Two sections were considered by the Commissioner. The first section was IHTA 1984 s 171. This provides that changes occurring in an estate as a result of death must be taken into account in valuing an asset. However, the section does not apply if the interest of the deceased terminated on death, or passed by succession. It was held that the section did not apply as the deceased's interest as tenant in common did not change as a result of his death. The interest passed to his PRs, and did not change its nature. The section did not apply, and the fact that on death W had rights to remain in the house which could be asserted against the daughters meant that the value had to be discounted.

It was also argued that the related property provisions in IHTA 1984 s161 applied. This provides that if spouses own assets of the same nature, and the value of their respective shares would be more valuable if treated as one holding, then the value of the respective shares is a proportion of the combined value. So if H owns 30% of the shares in a company, and W owns another 30%, the value of the each shareholding is one half of the value of a controlling shareholding, not the value of a 30% minority holding. The Commissioner considered that the section did not apply to shares in land.

The Commissioner held that the value had to be discounted because of the rights of the surviving spouse.

This case has been affirmed on appeal [[2004] EWHC 1720 (Ch)], but not as far as the Commissioner's findings on valuation were concerned. It was for the Lands Tribunal to decide the value of the half share. At the time of writing, there has been no reported decision as to the market value; presumably HMRC has agreed this with the husband's executors.

One disadvantage of this idea is that if house prices increase, when the children sell, which will usually be on the death of the surviving spouse, they will not be able to claim private residence exemption for CGT purposes. This is only a problem if house prices increase dramatically, but it will not be a problem if they remain static.

Another disadvantage of this scheme is non tax. The children may try to enforce a sale of the property evicting the surviving parent. Sometimes it is not the children who are the trouble, but their spouses or partners. This will not necessarily be a problem with all children, and even if a child does try to enforce a sale, the child probably will not succeed because of the Trusts of Land and Appointment of Trustees Act 1996. The court would have regard to the purpose for which the house was purchased—to provide a home for the parents, and probably refuse to order a sale. However, it will be a big problem if a child becomes bankrupt. At the end of the day, it is not possible to prevent a trustee in bankruptcy enforcing a sale of the house—the court can only refuse to make an order in exceptional circumstances.

There may also be problems if the child gets involved in divorce proceedings, or predeceases the surviving parent. If a child predeceases, it is not known who they might leave the half share to, and if the child's estate is large enough, then IHT will be payable on the child's interest in the former matrimonial home.

One possible way round this is for the children to transfer their interest to hold or trust for the surviving spouse for life.

Example

S1 gives half share in house to the children then transfer the half share to trustees to hold or trust for the surviving spouse for life, remainder to the children.

The settlement created by the children will be subject to the relevant property regeme, and so the half share will not be part of the surviving spouses estate on death as far as IHT is concerned.

However, there will not be any free uplift to market value on the death of the surviving spouse as for a CGT is concerned for the half share vested in the trustees, and it may be that main residence exemption will not be available.

The children will be deemed to have made a chargeable disposal as far as IHT is concerned, and may not be prepared to create the trust. In addition, the settlement could be set aside on the bankruptcy of a child.

NRB DISCRETIONARY TRUST

Inheritance tax

25.6   This idea is a very simple one. All trusts are now going to be subject to the relevant property regime unless they are within the three exemptions—an immediate post death interest, a trust for a bereaved minor and a trust for a disabled person. There may be ten yearly or principal charges and exit or proportionate charges, but they cannot be more than 6 per cent. If the original legacy to the trustees of a discretionary trust is less than the NRB, the chances are that there will be no ten yearly charges or exit charges.

Both spouses make wills creating discretionary trusts, and ensure that whatever goes into the discretionary trust is within the NRB. There would also be a gift to the surviving spouse to take advantage of spouse exemption. With the great majority of clients, the house or their share in it is the largest asset. The personal representatives of the first spouse to die can appropriate the whole of or a proportion of the share of the first spouse to die in the matrimonial home in satisfaction of the NRB legacy. The assets in the discretionary trust are not necessarily lost to the surviving spouse. As long as the trustees of the discretionary trust agree, then all the assets could be given to the surviving spouse.

This is the disadvantage of this idea as many surviving spouses will not want to be at the mercy of the trustees, who will probably be the adult children. However, with the great majority of families, this will not be a problem. The children will be prepared to help the surviving parent if necessary.

The great advantage of this scheme is that no IHT payable on what is left in the trust on the death of the surviving spouse.

It has been suggested that the scheme could fall foul of s 144 of the Inheritance Tax Act 1984. Section 144 in effect provides that if there is a discretionary trust in a will, and there is an appointment out of the discretionary trust within two years of death, then it is treated as if the deceased had disposed of the assets in accordance with whatever appointment is made by the trustees. It is possible that if the interest or part of the interest of the first spouse to die in the matrimonial home is appropriated in satisfaction of the NRB legacy, and the trustees acquiesce in the surviving spouse remaining in occupation, then HMRC might argue that there has been an appointment out in favour of the surviving spouse so as to give him or her a life interest in the interest of the first spouse to die. That interest would be an immediate post death interest, and accordingly the whole of the house would be subject to IHT on the death of the surviving spouse.

Section 144 is triggered by "an event". If the trustees of the NRB discretionary trust merely acquiesce in the surviving spouse living in the former matrimonial home, it is arguable that it is not an event. However, it is probably better to err on the cautious side, and to wait two years from the date of death of the first spouse before making the appropriation.

Capital gains tax

25.7   When the first spouse dies, there will not be any liability for CGT. Instead, there will be a free uplift to market value. The trustees will be deemed to acquire the assets in the trust at market value as that date of death of the first spouse. If they sell the assets within the trust for more than the market value at the date of death, then they may incur a liability for CGT. If the trustees decide to hand out any of the assets in the trust, they will be deemed to dispose of those assets at market value on the day when they hand them out. However, if the trustees and beneficiaries agree, any gain can be held over whatever the nature of the assets that the trustees are handing out. So if the trustees are holding shares in Marks and Spencer and decide to hand them out, that will be a deemed disposal at market value on the day when they hand them out, and if they have increased in value there is a potential liability for CGT on the trustees. However, if both the trustees and beneficiaries agree, then any gain can be held over.

If the trustees are holding a house as part of the trust assets, it is possible that the trustees would be able to claim private residence exemption if they sell the house during the lifetime of the surviving spouse. There is of course no problem as far as the interest of the surviving spouse is concerned—the surviving spouse can claim private residence exemption. However, it is possible that s 225 does not apply in this scenario; please see para 25.14 for a discussion of this aspect. These CGT problems will only arise if house prices increase. If they remain static, or do not increase very much each year, there should not be any problem.

Income tax

25.8   Another disadvantage of this idea is income tax.

The trustees of a discretionary trust are liable to income tax at 40 per cent on all income received apart from dividend income where they will be liable to income tax at the 32.5 per cent.

If the trustees pay any income to a beneficiary, the beneficiary gets a tax credit for income tax paid by the trustees.

NIL RATE BAND DISCRETIONARY TRUST, RESIDUE TO SPOUSE; TRUSTEES CAN ACCEPT IOU OR CHARGE FOR NRB LEGACY

25.9   This is a very popular way of drafting wills, and has the effect of utilising the NRB of both spouses without tying up the property of the deceased spouse so that the other spouse cannot use it freely.

Both wills create a NRB discretionary trust, and the trustees have power to accept an IOU from the surviving spouse for the amount of the legacy, and the executors have power to impose a charge.

Example

W gives a NRB legacy to the trustees of a discretionary trust, the residue to the spouse.

The trustees are empowered to accept an IOU from the surviving spouse or impose a charge for the NRB legacy.

W dies.

The trustees of the NRB discretionary trust accept an IOU from H.

H dies leaving an estate of £1,000,000.

It is hoped that the IOU for the NRB legacy will be deductible.

Assuming the NRB is always £300,000, H's taxable estate will be reduced to £400,000 − £100,000 minus the IOU for £300,000 minus H's NRB of £300,000.

The debt can be index linked, or might be expressed as a proportion of the value of the property. It is probably better if it is secured by a charge because an IOU might prove to be worthless on the death of the surviving spouse, and also to avoid stamp duty land tax; please see para for a discussion of stamp duty land tax.

Inheritance tax

25.10   No IHT will be payable on the death of the first spouse because the legacy is within the NRB, and the residue is exempt by virtue of the spouse exemption; on the death of the second spouse IHT will be payable, but the value of the death estate of the surviving spouse will be reduced by the IOU or charge, and the surviving spouse's own NRB. In effect, the NRB of the first spouse to die has been preserved.

Possible problems

25.11

(*a*)   There is a possibility of a charge on each tenth anniversary, and also on distributions of capital. The amount of IHT payable should be small as the rate of IHT payable on the tenth anniversary is 6per cent once the NRB has been exceeded. However, with all NRB discretionary trusts, it will be necessary to value all the assets in the trust on the first tenth anniversary of the death of the first spouse, and every subsequent tenth anniversary. In order to determine the rate of tax, it is necessary to know the NRB for the tax year when the tenth anniversary falls. Assuming that the settlor has not created any other discretionary trusts in the seven years prior to death, or created any other settlement in the will apart from a life interest trust for the surviving spouse, and that there has been no payments of capital from the trust in the ten years leading up to the tenth anniversary, the NRB will be intact. If the value of the assets within the trust is within the NRB, then no IHT will be payable. If the value of the assets is in excess of the NRB, then IHT is payable at 6 per cent on the value above the NRB.

The NRB usually increases at slightly more than the rate of inflation each year, so if the IOU or charge is just for the amount of the NRB at the date of death, there will be no ten-yearly charge as the IOU or charge will be within the NRB. However, if the IOU or charge is linked to the RPI or CPI or expressed as a proportion of the value of the house, or there are other assets in the trust, then there is a possibility that the IOU or charge and the other assets will be worth more than the NRB on the tenth anniversary. If it is, IHT is payable on the excess over the NRB, or what is left of it.

Example

The IOU is for the NRB—it should be within the NRB for the tax year in which the tenth anniversary falls.

If the IOU is linked to the RPI, or expressed as a proportion of the value of the house, and is worth £500,000 on the tenth anniversary, IHT is payable at 6 per cent once the NRB has been exceeded.

Thus if the NRB is £400,000 in the tax year in which the tenth anniversary falls, IHT at 6 per cent will be payable on £100,000, assuming that nothing has reduced the NRB.

(*b*)   Do not create another settlement in the will unless it is in favour of the spouse. Both settlements will be treated as related, and may adversely affect the IHT payable on the settlements.

(*c*)   If the trustees did not impose any obligation on the surviving spouse to pay interest at a commercial rate, there was a risk that HMRC would argue that he or she had an interest in possession. The trustees have in effect made a loan to the surviving spouse of the amount of the IOU or charge. If the surviving spouse did not have to pay interest, then the surviving spouse is obtaining the loan free of charge, and therefore had an interest in possession in the amount of the IOU. This meant that when the surviving spouse died, he or she would be deemed for IHT purposes to have disposed of the value of the NRB.

If the IOU or charge does bear interest, it will have income tax consequences if the trustees insist on the payment of the interest, and so it may be best if the trustees do not insist on the payment of interest each year, but instead roll the interest up and claim the rolled-up interest as a debt due from the estate of the surviving spouse reducing the estate of the surviving spouse as far as IHT is concerned. There would then be a liability for income tax on the rolled-up interest. Alternatively the trustees could waive the interest. This aspect is discussed in more detail in para.

Another possibility is to index link the loan, or express it as a proportion of the value of the house.

This point may not be open to HMRC in the light of the changes to the taxation of trusts in the Finance Act 2006. All trusts will now be subject to the relevant property regime unless they are immediate post death interests, trusts for bereaved minors or trusts for disabled persons.

These trusts are clearly not immediate post death interests or trusts for disabled persons which are the only two trusts left where the beneficiary will be deemed to have an interest in possession.

(*d*)   There is also a problem if the surviving spouse has made gifts to the first spouse to die.

The problem is that there are anti-avoidance provisions in the Finance Act 1986 designed to counteract artificial debts. A debt is not deductible if the consideration for it consisted of property derived from the deceased. These provisions apply if one spouse has made gifts to the other. This is quite common with clients in their seventies and eighties—40 or 50 years ago it was common for houses to be vested in the name of the husband, whereas now most houses are vested in the joint names of spouses or cohabitees. As times changed, the husband might have transferred the house into joint names. If the spouses then make wills creating NRB discretionary trusts, and giving the trustees power to accept an IOU, and the wife dies first, the HMRC may claim that this is an artificial debt. The artificial debt rules may also apply where there is a discrepancy in wealth between the spouses, and the wealthy spouse has transferred assets to the other spouse, and the wealthy spouse is the survivor. They could also apply where one spouse has inherited assets, and used them to redeem the mortgage on the matrimonial home if that spouse is the survivor.

Example

Assume NRB is £300,000.

H has given a half share in the house to W.

Assume that the half share is worth £300,000, and that W has no other assets.

W dies having created a NRB discretionary trust in her will, and conferred appropriate powers on the trustees.

H gives the trustees an IOU for the NRB legacy.

The executors vest W's assets, the half share in the house, in H.

The trustees have made him a loan of £300,000 in consideration of the transfer of W's assets to him.

As these assets came from H originally, the debt is artificial, and cannot be deducted from H's estate on his death.

In Phizackerley v HMRC [2007] UKSPC SPC00591 on his retirement in 1992, the deceased and his wife purchased a house for £150,000. The house was conveyed to them as joint tenants. There was a mortgage of £30,000 which was repaid in 1994. The wife did not have any paid employment throughout the marriage, and accordingly all the funds for the house were provided by the deceased.

In May 1996 the joint tenancy was severed. In the same month, the wife executed a will creating a NRB discretionary trust and giving the trustees power to take an IOU.

The wife died in April 2000, and the deceased promised to pay the trustees of the NRB discretionary trust £150,000 (index linked). All the assets of the wife were then vested in the deceased.

The deceased died in July 2002. His personal representative sought to deduct the IOU, which was now worth £156,013 from his estate.

HMRC contended that this was an artificial debt within s 103 of the Finance Act 1986 and was not deductible. The Special Commissioner held that this was correct.

It was argued on behalf of the personal representative that the artificial debt rules did not apply as the gift to the wife was not a transfer of value because it came within s 11 of the Inheritance Act 1984 being a disposition for the maintenance of the family.

The Special Commissioner held that the gift of the half share was not for the maintenance of the wife with the result that the IOU was not deductible from the estate of the husband. Note that there would have been no problem if the husband had died first.

The artificial debt rules only apply if it is the deceased who has created the debt. In view of this, it has been suggested that the way round this is to give the executors power to vest assets in a beneficiary subject to a charge for the NRB legacy. As it is the executors who have created the charge, there is no problem with the artificial debt rules. However, this could cause another problem if the surviving spouse wants to move house. The surviving spouse could agree with the trustees that he or she will grant another charge on the new house. However, this could trigger the anti-avoidance provisions contained in s 103 of the Finance Act 1986. The surviving spouse is creating a new charge in place of one created by the trustees. The consideration for the original charge was provided by property derived from the surviving spouse—therefore the anti-avoidance provisions are triggered.

If this is likely to be a problem, the residue should be given to trustees to hold on trust for the surviving spouse for life. The residue would include the equitable interest of the first spouse to die in the house.

The legal estate will vest in the surviving spouse, and if the surviving spouse wants to sell, he or she can do so by appointing a new trustee as two are required to give a valid receipt for capital unless a restriction has been entered at the Land Registry protecting the interests of the trustees of the NRB discretionary trust. It may be that the surviving spouse will be able to purchase his or her new house with his or her half share of the proceeds of sale and other assets, and so there is no problem. The trustees of the NRB discretionary trust will receive enough of the proceeds of sale of the house to enable them to discharge the charge, Those proceeds can either be invested or distributed. If that is not the case, then the trustees will have to permit the surviving spouse to utilise the half share of the proceeds of sale or at least part of it. The trustees of the residue will acquire an equitable interest in the new house, and can give the trustees of the NRB discretionary trust a charge over the equitable interest in the new property. As it is the trustees and not the surviving spouse who have created the charge, the anti-avoidance provisions should not be triggered.

Example

H has given a half share in the matrimonial home to W.

W dies having created a NRB discretionary trust in her will.

W appointed C1 and C2 as executors, and H, C1 and C2 as trustees of the NRB discretionary trust.

The residue has been given to C1 and C2 to hold on trust for H for life, then to C1 and C2.

C1 and C2 will take W's equitable interest in the matrimonial home, and can create a charge in favour of H, C1 and C2.

If H wants to move house, he can sell by appointing another trustee.

C1 and C2 will acquire an equitable interest in the new house, and can then give H, C1 and C2 a charge over their equitable interest in the new house.

In Phizackerley if the wife's executors had imposed a charge on the wife's equitable interest in the house, and vested the equitable interest in the husband, it may be that there would have been no problem with the artificial debt rules as it was not the husband who was creating the charge but the wife's executors. In addition there would have been no problem if the husband had died first.

Another simple solution to the problem might be for the executors of the first spouse to die to vest the equitable interest of the first spouse in the matrimonial home in the names of the trustees of the NRB discretionary trust. If the surviving spouse wanted to move house, then the trustees could join in the sale of the former matrimonial home and the purchase of a new house. The trustees would get an equitable interest in the new house of the surviving spouse.

There may be problems with this idea. The first problem is s 144 of the Inheritance Tax Act 1984.

This provides that if there is a discretionary trust in the will, and there is an event which would give rise to a charge to IHT within two years of the death of the testator, it is treated as if the testator had disposed of the assets in accordance with the event. As with deeds of variation within two years of death, the event is read back into the will. An appointment out of a discretionary trust in a will within two years of death is an event which would normally give rise to a charge to IHT. Accordingly, an appointment out of the trust within two years of the death of the testator is treated as if the testator had disposed of the assets in accordance with whatever appointment the trustees make. If the executors of the first spouse to die vest the equitable interest in the matrimonial home of that spouse in the trustees of the NRB discretionary trust, and the trustees acquiesce in the surviving spouse living in the house, does that constitute an appointment out of the trust? If it did, then the surviving spouse would have an immediate post death interest in the half share of the first spouse to die, and that would be part of his or her estate on death.

This is a grey area, but it is possible that HMRC will accept that mere acquiescence by the trustees in the surviving spouse remaining in occupation of the matrimonial home is not an appointment, or an event, within s 144. However, there is clearly a risk that HMRC might take the point (see Questions by STEP/CIOT and answers from HMRC to Schedule 20 Finance Act 2006 (January 2007).

The solution may be to wait two years from the death of the first spouse before vesting the equitable interest of the first spouse into the names of the trustees of the NRB discretionary trust. There can be then no question of falling foul of s 144.

With both these ideas for getting around the anti-avoidance rules to do with artificial debts, it may also be that when the house is sold, the trustees of the NRB discretionary trust will not be able to claim private residence exemption for any gain accruing to them. Section 225 of the Taxation of Chargeable Gains Act provides that if trustees are holding a house, and under the terms of the settlement, it becomes the principal private residence of that beneficiary, when the house is sold, the trustees can claim private residence exemption. However, there is a considerable element of doubt as to whether the trustees holding an equitable interest in a house where the surviving spouse has the other equitable interest have power to permit the surviving spouse to live in the former matrimonial home. If the trustees do not have such power, then s 225 does not apply, and accordingly the trustees will not be able to claim private residence exemption on any gain on the half share vested in them.

On the other hand, if the residue is an immediate post death interest for the benefit of the surviving spouse, when the surviving spouse dies there will be a free uplift for CGT purposes of all the assets in the trust. Accordingly, if the half share of the first spouse to die is vested in the names of the trustees, when the surviving spouse dies, no CGT will be payable, but instead the remainder men, usually the adult children, will acquire that half share at market value as at the date of death of the surviving spouse.

Another possible way of implementing these NRB discretionary trusts is to wait until two years have elapsed from the death of the first spouse and then appoint the half share of the house on a life interest trust for the benefit of the surviving spouse. As it is not an immediate post-death interest, HMRC cannot argue that there is an interest in possession. Why wait two years? If the trustees make the appointment within two years of the death of the first spouse, then the appointment will be read back into the will under s144. It would then be taxed as if it was an immediate post death interest with the consequence that the assets in the trust would be subject to IHT on the death of the surviving spouse. The surviving spouse can live in the house, and when the surviving spouse dies, the house will not be part of the surviving spouse is estate for IHT purposes.

As with all these ideas, there are disadvantages. The first disadvantage is that if house prices increase, there is a possibility of a 10-yearly or principal charge to IHT. This is of course only a problem if house prices increase, and IHT will probably only be payable on the value over and above the NRB for the tax year when the 10th anniversary falls. In addition, the rate of IHT is very low—6 per cent. This compares very favourably with the rate of IHT which would have been payable if the surviving spouse had an interest in possession in the house.

The second disadvantage is that when the surviving spouse dies, there will not be any free uplift to market value. There may also be a problem with private residence exemption as far as the trustees are concerned if the house is sold; this issue was considered above.

The author considers that the real difficulty posed by Phizackerley is to know how far HMRC will go in alleging gifts as in many marriages there will have been gifts from one spouse to the other. It may be that the spouses will have had a joint bank or building society account, and paid all their earnings into that account. If the surviving spouse has earned more than the other, will HMRC seek to invoke the artificial debt rules if the one who has earned more is the one who survives? Will HMRC seek to invoke the rules if the surviving spouse has inherited assets from the estates of parents, and used them to pay off the mortgage on the matrimonial home?

For a discussion of whether the surviving spouse should be one of the executors, please see (f) below.

(e)   The loan should not become statute barred. This means that every six years the surviving spouse should acknowledge that the loan is still outstanding—or every twelve years if the IOU is under seal. However, it may be that time does not begin to run against the trustees until there is a demand for repayment (See Section 6 Limitation Act

1980) and if the surviving spouse is one of the trustees the surviving spouse or his or her estate may not be allowed to take this point.

(f) It may be that the surviving spouse should not be the sole trustee. This is because you cannot contract with yourself. However, if there are other trustees, this is not a problem.

If the surviving spouse has made gifts to the first spouse to die, and it is proposed to impose a charge, it is probably best if the surviving spouse is not one of the trustees or personal representatives who create the charge. This is to avoid any danger that HMRC might argue that s 103 has been triggered. On the other hand, if the surviving spouse is one of the executors or trustees, it could be argued that the surviving spouse is not imposing the charge himself or herself; instead it is the executors or trustees collectively who are imposing the charge.

In order to avoid the question of whether someone can create an interest in favour of himself, the trustees of the NRB discretionary trust and the residue should not be exactly the same. At least one trustee should be different.

(g) Some assets must be put into the trust. It seems that HMRC may object if nothing is put into the trust other than the IOU or charge. The trustees must therefore hold some assets other than the IOU or charge. It is probably prudent to inject into the discretionary trust as much as the surviving spouse can afford to inject; it is not necessarily lost to the surviving spouse as the trustees can pay it out if necessary.

Another reason for putting assets into the trust is to fund administration expenses, and the payment of any ten yearly charge to IHT. If the trustees only have an IOU or a charge, then how do they pay the cost of administering the trust, or a ten yearly charge? It is much simpler if they have some other assets in the trust, and can use them to pay the administration expenses or ten yearly charge.

In addition, these trusts must work so far as the trustees hold cash or other assets. This point has perhaps become more important since Phizackerly.

(h) If the deceased leaves property qualifying for either agricultural property relief or business property relief, and leaves this type of will, the value of that property may be attributed to both the NRB legacy and the residue. This will happen if the legacy is stated to be the NRB or whatever is left of the NRB.

So if a testator has assets which could qualify for agricultural property relief or business property relief, then the will should make it clear whether or not that property is to be included in the legacy to the trustees of the discretionary trust.

(*i*)   What is the position if the matrimonial home is mortgaged?

Presumably any charge can only be for the value of the equity of redemption.

So if the matrimonial home is worth £500,000, and there is a mortgage of £300,000, any charge could only be for the equity of redemption - £200,000.

(*j*)   What is the position if the estate of the first spouse to die is less than the NRB? It is contentious as to whether it is possible to implement the NRB discretionary trust when the estate of the first spouse to die is less than the NRB.

It is the view of the author that if the combined estates of spouses are only marginally above the NRB, it is not worth bothering with these NRB discretionary trusts. However, in case some client does think that it is worthwhile, then perhaps precedents should be modified so that there is some residue left. It may be desirable to limit the NRB legacy to a percentage of the residuary estate with a maximum of the NRB in case the residue does not exceed the NRB or alternatively it may be that the trustees of the nil rate band discretionary trust will have power to fix the amount of the nil rate band legacy so that they could determine that the legacy, is for example, 90% of the estate.

(*k*)   It has been suggested that the will should not contain a survivorship clause. This is because s 92 IHTA 1984 provides that where under the terms of a will...property is held for any person on condition that he survives another for a specified period of not more than six months, this Act shall apply as if the dispositions taking effect at the end of the period...had had effect from the beginning of the period.

Under s 92 it is the beneficiary who receives the gift who must satisfy the survivorship condition. So if there is a will where spouses give everything to each other subject to a survivorship clause not exceeding six months, and the survivor survives for the survivorship period, it is treated as if the gift takes effect from the commencement of the period, from the moment of death of the first spouse. In effect the survivorship clause is ignored, and it is treated as if the surviving spouse had been entitled to the legacy the moment the first spouse died.

If s 92 did not exist, who would be entitled to the gift during the survivorship period? Whoever was entitled to the estate after the surviving spouse would be entitled to the gift to the surviving spouse between the date of death and the date when the condition was satisfied. In the traditional type of will, this means the children. When the surviving spouse satisfies the survivorship condition, then it is the children who would be deemed to have made the gift to the surviving spouse if it was not for s 92.

It is the trustees of the NRB discretionary trust who are the beneficiaries of the legacy. So if there is a gift of the NRB legacy to the trustees, and the survivorship clause is that the trustees must survive for 28 days, if they do, there is no problem as s 92 applies, and the gift is effective from the date of death of the first spouse.

However, if the NRB discretionary trust is subject to the surviving spouse surviving for 28 days, it is arguable that that gift does not come within s 92 as the NRB legacy is to the trustees. If s 92 does not apply to NRB discretionary trusts, then when the first spouse dies, the legacy would fall into the residuary estate, and either the surviving spouse or the children would be entitled depending on the terms of the residuary gift.

However, when the condition is satisfied, for IHT purposes, the gift would not be read back into the will, so the surviving spouse or children would be deemed to have made a chargeable disposal of the NRB. If the children were entitled to the residuary estate, then it may not be that serious as the NRB of the first spouse to die will not have been lost.

Example

S1 creates NRB discretionary trust subject to a survivorship clause.

Residue to surviving spouse S2.

The argument is that s 92 does not apply if it is the surviving spouse who must satisfy the survivorship clause and not the trustees. If it is the surviving spouse, the consequence is that when S1 dies, S2 will be entitled to all the assets in the trust. If S2 satisfies the survivorship clause, then the NRB discretionary trust comes into effect. For IHT purposes S2 will be deemed to have made a chargeable disposal, and the NRB of the first spouse to die will have been lost.

If it is the children who are entitled to the residuary estate, then the consequences are not so great as the NRB of the first spouse to die will have been preserved.

With regard to the residue, one of the reasons for including a survivorship clause in a gift of the residue to the spouse was to preserve the NRB of the first spouse to die in case the spouses died in quick succession. From this point of view, a survivorship clause for the residue is unnecessary as the NRB of the first spouse to die has been utilised in the NRB discretionary trust.

As far as the default beneficiaries are concerned, a survivorship clause might save some IHT if both spouses and the other beneficiaries, usually a child or children died in quick succession. Otherwise, the child's estate will include what he or she has inherited from parents.

NRB discretionary trusts after the Finance Act 2006

25.12 As all trusts apart from trusts for disabled persons, trusts for bereaved minors and immediate post death interests are now subject to the relevant property regime it is impossible for HMRC to argue that a beneficiary under a discretionary trust has an interest in possession for IHT purposes.

It would therefore appear to be safe to vest the interest of the first spouse to die in the matrimonial home in the trustees, although there is a possible problem with s 144 of the Inheritance Act 1984.

However, if the house is sold, it could be that the trustees will not be able to claim private residence exemption for their interest. In addition, there will not be a free uplift to market value on the death of the surviving spouse. If the trustees appoint their interest in the house to a beneficiary, that could give rise to an exit charge as far as IHT is concerned and it would be a deemed disposal at market value for CGT purposes, but if the trustees and beneficiary agree, then hold over relief would be available.

If no problem with the artificial debt rules:

Put as much of the cash/investments of the first spouse to die into the names of the trustees as possible.

Vest the half share of the first spouse to die in the matrimonial home in the surviving spouse subject to a charge in favour of the trustees. Then there will be a free uplift to market value on the death of the surviving spouse, and if the surviving spouse sells, main residence exemption will be available.

If problem with the artificial debt rules:

Put as much of the cash/investments of the first spouse to die into the names of the trustees as possible.

Tie the residue up in a life interest trust, or vest the half share of the first spouse to die in the matrimonial home in the trustees of the NRB discretionary trust although be wary of S144 of the Inheritance Tax Act 1984.

However, as far as CGT is concerned, there will be no uplift to market value of the assets in the trust. This is only a problem if the assets increase in value substantially. When the trustees sell they may be not able to claim private residence exemption for the time when the surviving spouse was living in the house.

If there are other assets in the trust, and these produce income then the trustees will have to pay income tax at 40 per cent on all income apart from dividends, 32.5 per cent on dividends.

There is also the control issue—most surviving spouses want to have control of the house. If the half share of the first spouse to die is vested in the names of trustees, then the surviving spouse loses control.

CGT

25.13   If the trustees sell assets subject to the trust for more than the purchase price, or, if the assets were given to the trustees, for more than the market value at the date of transfer, there is a potential liability to CGT. There will be no deaths to extinguish liability.

If the IOU was linked to the RPI or CPI or expressed as a percentage of the value of the house, then, if it is worth more than what it was issued for, on the death of the surviving spouse there may be a liability to CGT or income tax (see **25.15** below). It should be noted that views differ as to whether there is such a liability.

The problem with private residence relief

25.14   As mentioned earlier, if the equitable half share of the first spouse to die in the matrimonial home is vested in the trustees of the NRB discretionary trust, it is possible that when the house is sold, the trustees will not be able to claim private residence relief.

The reason for this is that s 225 of the Taxation of Chargeable Gains Act 1992 provides that where trustees are holding a house, and a beneficiary is entitled to occupy it under the terms of the settlement, and does so as their main residence, then if the house is sold, the trustees can claim private residence exemption for the time the beneficiary was living in the house as the beneficiary's main residence.

Section 12 of the Trusts of Land and Appointment of Trustees Act 1996 provides that where a beneficiary is entitled to an interest in possession under a settlement, they are entitled to live in any house forming part of the trust assets.

The Taxation of Chargeable Gains Act 1992 requires that the beneficiary should be entitled to occupy the house under the terms of the settlement.

Section 12 of the 1996 Act makes it clear that the member of a class of beneficiaries under a discretionary trust has no right to live in a house forming part of the assets of the trust.

Do the trustees of the NRB discretionary trust holding the equitable interest of the first spouse to die in the matrimonial home have power to agree that the surviving spouse can live in the former matrimonial home when the surviving spouse is entitled to live there because they are co-owners?

That is the issue here, and opinions are divided as to whether it is possible for the members of the class of a discretionary trust where the trustees are holding an equitable interest in a house to be given a right to live in it. If they can, then it will be possible to claim private residence exemption. If they cannot be given the right, then it will not be possible to claim private residence exemption.

Income tax

25.15   If the trustees accept an IOU from the surviving spouse, and no interest is payable, then there will not be any income on which income tax will be payable.

If there is any income, the trustees will pay income tax at 40 per cent, but if the income is paid to a beneficiary who is not a basic or higher rate taxpayer, the beneficiary will be able to recover the tax paid as long as their taxable income does not exceed their personal allowance. A beneficiary who is a basic rate taxpayer will be able to recover the difference between the basic rate and the 40 per cent, as long as the income received from the trust does not mean that they become a higher rate taxpayer. A beneficiary who is already a higher rate taxpayer will not be liable for any more tax, but will not be able to recover any.

If the surviving spouse is a higher rate taxpayer, and pays the interest out of income taxed at the higher rate, the combined rate of tax will be 80 per cent. If the surviving spouse is not a higher rate taxpayer, if interest is paid, the combined rate will be 62 per cent.

If the interest is rolled up, it could be claimed as a debt due from the estate of the surviving spouse. The trustees will then have to pay income tax at 40 per cent, but if the interest is paid to a beneficiary who is a non-taxpayer, or not a higher rate taxpayer, it will be possible to recover at least part of the income tax.

If there is any income, it should not be mandated to the surviving spouse within two years of the death of the first spouse as if it is HMRC may argue that the surviving spouse has an immediate post-death interest.

The IOU could be a relevant discounted security within FA 1996 Schedule 13. This applies where the issue price of a security is less than the redemption proceeds.

Example

The IOU is for £300,000, and is linked to the RPI.

It is worth £400,000 on the death of the surviving spouse.

There is a possibility of a charge to income tax under this section on some of the difference between the amount for which the IOU was issued, and the amount it yielded at the end of the day, which will be the responsibility of the trustees of the NRB discretionary trust.

Not everyone agrees that these IOUs are deep discounted securities

If they are not deep discounted securities, HMRC might seek to charge the increase in value to income tax on the basis that it is interest. It is the payment for the loan, and if it is viewed in that light, then it is subject to income tax.

If the increase in value is not subject to income tax, then there is a risk that HMRC may seek to charge the increase in value to CGT. Section 251 of the Taxation of Chargeable Gains Act 1992 appears to exempt debts from CGT. However, it could be argued that the IOU is a piece of property which has gone up in value, and that when it is repaid that the increase in value is subject to CGT. If the increase in value is not that great, there should be no problem as it should be covered by the annual exemption available to trustees.

Stamp duty land tax

25.16   Is the IOU subject to SDLT?

Is any charge subject to SDLT?

This has been a vexed question, and opinions have differed.

However, the HMRC have produced a statement saying in effect that SDLT is payable in various circumstances. Is this correct?

SDLT charges a land transaction. A land transaction is any acquisition of a chargeable interest. What is a chargeable interest? It is an estate, interest, right or power in or over land in the UK.

With the NRB discretionary trust scheme coupled with the power to accept an IOU, it is arguable that what is happening is that the executors are in effect selling the assets of the first spouse to die to the survivor in return for an IOU. As the assets of the first spouse to die will include the interest of that spouse in the matrimonial home, it is arguable that there is a land transaction. This view is not universally held.

The HMRC statement provides that SDLT is chargeable in the following circumstances:

1. Where the PRs accept a promise by the surviving spouse to pay, and transfer the house to the surviving spouse in consideration of that promise.

2. The trustees of the NRB legacy accept a promise to pay in satisfaction of the legacy, and land is transferred to the surviving spouse in consideration of the spouse liability on the promise.

3. Where the PRs transfer land to the surviving spouse, and the spouse charges the property with the amount of the legacy.

However, no SDLT is payable if the PRs charge the land with the NRB legacy, and the PRs and the trustees of the NRB legacy agree that there is no personal liability on the owner of the land for the time being.

How does this work? It is possible to have charge over land where there is no personal liability on anyone. Presumably the trustees will not be able to enforce the charge until the house is sold or the surviving spouse dies as otherwise they would be making the surviving spouse personally liable.

On what consideration do you pay the SDLT? It is the amount for which the IOU or charge is given.

It has been suggested in para 25.11 (c) that an obligation should be imposed on the surviving spouse to pay interest at a commercial rate in order to prevent HMRC arguing that there was an interest in possession. Alternatively, you can link the IOU to the CPI or RPI, or express it as a proportion of the value of the house. This may not be a point open to HMRC. However, it may be wise to assume that it could still be a point open to HMRC. It would be rather odd to have a charge which states that there is no personal liability on the surviving spouse, and then goes on to impose a liability to pay interest at a commercial rate If the trustees and the personal representatives agree to impose a charge and state that there is to be no personal liability on the surviving spouse, and then the surviving spouse agrees in a separate document to pay interest at a commercial rate, HMRC might argue that there was a land transaction. The promise to pay interest was given in return for the transfer of the former matrimonial home to the surviving spouse, and therefore there is a land transaction.

Alternatively, the personal representatives and trustees of the NRB discretionary trust could agree that the charge was to be linked to the RPI or CPI, or expressed as a proportion of the value of the house. In the view of the author, it is best to link it to the RPI or CPI. The reasons for this are that it should avoid any argument by HMRC that there is an interest in possession in the IOU. In addition, there should not be a major problem, if any, with ten yearly charges. And further if there is a CGT liability if the charge increases in value, it may be covered by the annual exemption for CGT purposes.

Another issue is that the value of the half share in the house may be less than the NRB. In that situation there will have to be a charge for the value of the half share imposed by the executors and trustees with no liability on the surviving spouse, and the surviving spouse will then have to give an IOU for the balance of the NRB.

Example

S1 and S2 execute NRB discretionary trust wills.

S1 dies.

Half share in matrimonial home is worth £150,000.

The executors of S1 can create a charge for the amount of the value of the half share over the half share. The charge must state that there is no personal liability on the S2 to repay the charge. If S2 then gives an IOU for the balance of the NRB it is arguable that there is no land transaction as the IOU is being given in return for the transfer to S2 of S1's cash and investments. As long as the IOU is drafted in these terms, that it is being given in return for the transfer of the non house assets, then hopefully no SDLT will be payable.

What is the value of S2's share? Is it a mathematical half of the full market value, or should there be a discount because the surviving spouse is entitled to remain in occupation? This is a matter for the valuers, but there should be some discount off the full market value.

Another issue is whether the executors and trustees of the NRB discretionary trust should be the same people. If they are, can they impose a charge in their favour? The argument that they cannot do so is because you cannot enter into a contract with yourself. However, what is happening is that the executors/trustees are imposing a charge on the half share in the matrimonial home which they are going to vest in the surviving spouse. It is not as if the executors and trustees are entering into a contract. In the circumstances it is probably best if the executors and trustees are not exactly the same—either appoint an additional trustee of the NRB discretionary trust, or one trustee can retire.

It has been suggested that you can avoid SDLT by creating the NRB discretionary trust in a deed of variation. It is certainly true that deeds of variation do not involve any SDLT liability. The SDLT exemption only applies if there is no consideration in money or money's worth. If the correct analysis of these NRB discretionary trusts is that it is a sale of the interest of the first spouse to die in return for the IOU, in the view of the author there is consideration.

Conveyancing

25.17   If the surviving spouse has granted a legal charge over the whole of the legal estate in favour of the trustees of the NRB discretionary trust, there is no problem. The legal charge can be registered in the usual manner, and accordingly the trustees of the NRB discretionary trust are secure.

However, if the executors/trustees of the first spouse to the have created a charge over the equitable interest of that spouse, that charge by its nature must be equitable. How can that equitable charge be protected? It is clear from the guidance notes issued by the Land Registry that such a charge cannot be protected by a notice. The correct way to proceed is to protect equitable charge by means of a restriction.

The problem with this is that a restriction in Form A does not offer much protection to the trustees of the NRB discretionary trust. The restriction in effect provides that the property can be sold if the proceeds are paid to two trustees.The surviving spouse will be the sole trustee of the legal estate of the former matrimonial home. If the surviving spouse wanted to defeat the trust, then the surviving spouse could appoint a cohabitee or his or her current spouse as trustee, sell the house and disappear with the proceeds. With the great majority of spouses, this will not be a problem. However, it may be a problem with a small minority.

If that is the case, it has been suggested that the trustees of the NRB discretionary trust should endeavour to get a restriction registered which requires the consent of the trustees to any sale of the house. Most Land Registries will not accept a restriction which requires the consent of the trustees for the time being of the NRB discretionary trust under the will of whoever it is. Almost certainly, they will require the restriction to name the trustees of the NRB discretionary trust.

Some Land Registries will not remove the existing tenant in common restriction when they have tried to enter a restriction protecting the trustees of the NRB discretionary trust. It seems that the way to get round this is to submit an RX3 and either a certificate from the conveyancer or a statutory declaration from the surviving spouse stating that they had become absolutely entitled to the property under the deceased's will, that the survivor has not encumbered their undivided share and that they have received no notice of an encumbrance upon the share of the deceased proprietor (see the posting on Trusts Discussion Forum on 14/02/07 by Kelly White).

The other way or protecting the interest of the trustees of the NRB is to arrange for them to be appointed as trustees of the legal estate.

Non-tax disadvantages

25.18   The surviving spouse is at the mercy of the trustees. This may or may not be a big disadvantage. If the children are the trustees of the NRB discretionary trust, there is no guarantee that they will agree to accept an IOU. They might insist on the cash. This could force the surviving spouse to sell the house.

Trustees must also act in the best interests of all the beneficiaries—is it in the best interests of all the beneficiaries to accept an IOU?

Trustees must also take advice about investments—what is the position if the advice is not to take an IOU, but instead to insist on cash, and invest it either directly or indirectly on the stock exchange? It may be very difficult to find anyone who is prepared to advise about whether or not to take an IOU.

Under the Trustee Act 2000, trustees are under a duty to review investments and take advice about them periodically, and they should meet regularly to consider whether they ought to call in the IOU, or enforce the charge, and invest the cash.

If they have accepted an IOU, and it is not supported by a charge, they may also need to consider whether there are going to be sufficient assets in the estate of the surviving spouse to satisfy the NRB legacy. If there are insufficient assets, this may eliminate any IHT charge, but could be a breach of trust as far as other beneficiaries are concerned.

There may also be problems in respect of a surviving spouse who is also an executor or trustee, but who will not co-operate with the other trustees; it may be that there would have to be an application to the court to remove such a trustee.

The distribution of the proceeds of the IOU on the death of the surviving spouse could also cause difficulties. It is not every family that will be able to agree on an equal division of the proceeds, and there may be some situations when it will be desirable to prolong the trust, for example if one child is mentally incapable.

What happens if the rules change?

25.19　　There is clearly a risk that the HMRC will attempt to stop these trusts. Should clients, therefore, be warned against making wills that include NRB discretionary trusts?

Clearly if the rules change, letters can be sent to all clients who have made such wills, advising them of the change and suggesting that the wills should be reviewed.

If the clients take no action, it will not necessarily be disastrous as presumably any change would prevent the deduction of the IOU or charge on the death of the surviving spouse.

In addition, it is possible to vary a will within two years of death, and the original testator will be treated as having disposed of the assets in accordance with the deed of variation.

Use could also be made of s 144 of the IHTA 1984. If a will creates a discretionary trust, and an appointment is made more than three months after death (in some circumstances the appointment can be made in the three months after death, but in practical terms the trustees will not be in a position to make an appointment within three months of death) but within two years of death, then the deceased is deemed to have disposed of the property in accordance with the appointment. This may mean that IHT is payable—if the appointment is in favour of children. However, if the appointment is in favour of a spouse who is domiciled in the UK, no IHT will be payable.

Section 144 does not apply to property in which the deceased had a life interest, or property in which the deceased reserved a benefit.

There is doubt as to whether an appointment can be made before the administration has been completed. Assuming that it can be, there is no reason why it should not be made prior to the application for a grant.

There is no special treatment for CGT purposes. Hold-over relief will only apply if the assets are business assets.

The CGT position may depend on whether the appointment is made before or after the completion of the administration.

Assume that it is an absolute appointment. It could be argued that until the administration is completed, the trustees only have a chose in action—the right to have the estate administered—which would have a nil base cost. Any appointment would be a deemed disposal at market value of that chose in action by the trustees. When the administration of the estate is completed, the personal representatives will vest the assets in the beneficiaries. The normal rule then applies—the beneficiaries will be deemed to have acquired the assets at market value as at the date of death. They are beneficiaries under the will.

On the other hand, if the administration has been completed the position is clear. The personal representatives vest the assets in the trustees, who are deemed to acquire assets at market value as at the date of death. If the trustees appoint an asset, shares or land, then the beneficiary will become absolutely entitled to those assets. This means that the trustees will be deemed to dispose of the assets at market value.

It is understood that the HMRC do not consider that there is a disposal of a chose in action in some situations (see Butterworths Wills, Probate and Administration Service, paras 937–940 footnote 7). However, it would seem to be prudent to wait until the administration has been completed if the trustees are the same as the executors, and for the trustees/executors to have a meeting resolving that they have become trustees, or appropriating to themselves the assets which they intend to appoint. If the executors and trustees are not the same, then clearly the assets to be appointed should be vested in the trustees before they make the appointment.

VARIATIONS

25.20   Although this book is not primarily about post-death variations, the author believes that there is considerable merit in spouses executing traditional wills whereby they give everything to each other subject to a survivorship clause, with a default gift to children and grandchildren. If the surviving spouse becomes absolutely entitled, then he or she can vary the will of the deceased spouse, possibly so as to create a NRB discretionary trust coupled with the power to accept an IOU. This suggestion is of course dependent on the continued ability to save tax by means of post-death variations.

Advantages/disadvantages of the charge route/IOU route

Advantages of the charge route:

25.21

1.   Security.

2. If PRs and trustees agree that there is to be no personal liability on the surviving spouse, then no SDLT is payable.

3. The charge route should be used if there is any problem with artificial debts.

Disadvantages of the charge route:

1. There may be insufficient equity.

2. Spouse may have to give an IOU for the balance.

It is possible that the value of the half share in the house will be less than the NRB.

In these circumstances, the surviving spouse will have to give an IOU for the balance.

Advantages of the IOU route

1. Can be for full amount of NRB less the value of any assets transferred to the trust.

2. Property not encumbered by any charge.

Disadvantages of IOU route

1. No security.

2. Possible problems with SDLT.

Implementation of NRB discretionary trusts

25.22   HMRC have made threatening noises about wanting NRB discretionary trusts to be implemented properly. It is unclear how real these threats are, but it is probably best to take them seriously.

On the death of the first spouse/cohabitee

*   Complete the administration of the estate

    This is particularly important if the trustees intend to break up the trust within two years of death as if they do so before they have the IOU, charge or assets vested in them HMRC may argue that there has been a disposal of a chose in action, with a nil base cost for CGT purposes.

- The trustees also need to have a meeting to decide on the balance between IOU/charge and other assets
- They should also take advice from someone who is qualified to advise about investments; this is probably inpracticable
- Arrange a meeting of the trustees to decide the balance between cash/assets and the IOU/charge
- Take advice with regard to any investments transferred to them
- Decide whether to proceed by the charge route or the IOU route
- Pay any SDLT

During the trust

Review investments and take advice

Under the Trustee Act 2000 trustees are under a duty to review the investments periodically and take advice. The review should take place at least once a year, and in certain circumstances more frequently than that. So strictly if trustees have taken an IOU/charge, they should take advice at least once a year as to whether they should continue to hold the IOU/charge, or whether they should get the cash and invest it on the stock exchange, or in some other type of investment, like bonds.

As with the duty to take advice when the settlement was first created, the trustees are faced with considerable difficulty if the advice is not to take the IOU/charge, but instead to get cash.

If the trustees are holding other assets, then of course they must take advice about those investments.

Have regular meetings

Ensuring that the surviving spouse has enough assets to satisfy the IOU?

What do the trustees do if they do not have a charge, and the surviving spouse is dissipating the assets of the surviving spouse? If this is happening, it may be that there will be nothing left to satisfy the IOU on the death of the surviving spouse. This will probably eliminate the IHT problem, but the trustees may be left with a headache.

The trustees owe a duty to the beneficiaries under the discretionary trust to preserve the assets of the trust. If there are insufficient assets to satisfy the IOU, then the trustees could be liable for breach of trust. If the trustees are family members, presumably the problem may be academic in that it is their own children who will be within the class of beneficiaries, and therefore they will not take action against their own parents. However, there is no guarantee that they will not take action. If this is likely to be a problem, then the trustees should take a charge to secure the amount due to them. If they do not, and it looks as if there may be insufficient assets to satisfy the IOU, then the trustees should call in the IOU immediately.

Completion of income tax return

If the trustees have an IOU which does not provide for interest, or if it does, they do not insist on the payment of the interest, there is no problem on this aspect. If the trustees hold other assets which are yielding income, then they will be liable to income tax at 40% on that income—32.5% if it is dividend income.

Every ten years

As it is a discretionary trust, there is a possibility of a charge every ten years. This will only apply if the value of the assets in the trust exceeds the NRB in the tax year in which the ten year anniversary falls. If it does, then the rate of IHT is not to be feared—it is only 6 per cent.

On death of surviving spouse

- Get in cash!
- Invest it?
- Distribute it?
- Settle outstanding liabilities

The PRs of the surviving spouse will be under a duty to pay the amount outstanding under the IOU/charge to the trustees. Once the trustees have the cash, they will then have to consider whether the discretionary trust is to come to an end, and the assets distributed to the beneficiaries, or whether the trust is to be continued.

With the great majority, the trustees will almost certainly decide to distribute the assets. However, there may be situations where it is not appropriate to distribute the assets immediately. What is the position if a member of the class of beneficiaries is in dire financial straits, and about to go bankrupt? It might be in the interests of all the beneficiaries under the trust to prevent the beneficiary going bankrupt.

Assume that there is only one child in dire financial straits, and his or her children within the class of beneficiaries. It might be in the interest of all of them to stop the child in dire financial straits going bankrupt. If child does go bankrupt, the family may be evicted from family home. On the other hand if anything given to the potential beneficiary is going to go straight to the creditors, and will not satisfy them so that the beneficiary is still made bankrupt, then there seems little point in giving the money to that beneficiary.

It may also be that a member of the class is in receipt of state benefits, or is in a care home. It may be that a large handout to such a member of the class will affect the entitlement to benefits.

If the trustees do decide to distribute, then they need to meet to consider whether to exercise their powers. They may decide to retain all the assets, in which even they will have to take advice about what they should be investing in, unless they are qualified to advise about investments.

If they do decide to distribute the assets, there is considerable room for argument as to who gets what, and that may cause trouble in some families. There may also be taxation liabilities which will have to be settled. There may be an exit charge as far as IHT is concerned. There may also be a charge to CGT, although hold over relief should be available. The beneficiaries will be absolutely entitled to the assets in the discretionary trust, and this will trigger a disposal at market value by the trustees. If that market value is higher than the price the trustees purchased the asset for, there is a potential liability for CGT. However, the trustees and the beneficiaries can elect that the gain should be held over, and because it is a discretionary trust, hold over relief applies whatever the nature of the assets involved.

Forms.

On creation.

If it is a lifetime settlement:

IHT 100.

IHT 100a.

IHT WS.

D31—D40.

41G.

64 – 8

If it is created by will:

IHT 200.

IHT WS.

41G.

64 – 8.

Every year.

Income tax return.

Every ten years.

IHT 100.

IHT 100d.

IHT WS.

D31—D40.

Exit or proportionate charge.

IHT 100.

IHT 100c.

IHT WS.

D31—D40.

The forms must generally be delivered by the end of the twelfth month after the transfer. Tax is due on six months after the end of the month in which the transfer was made. However, if the transfer was made between 6 April and 30 September, the tax is due on 30 April in the following year. Thus if the transfer was made between 6 April and 30 September, for example on 31 July, the tax is due by the next 30 April.

If the transfer was between 1 October and 5 April, the tax is due by the end of the sixth month after the transfer. So if the transfer was on 5 November, the tax must be paid by the end of the sixth month after the transfer—by the end of the following May.

SUMMARY

25.21   Consider the following ways of preserving the NRB of the first spouse to die:

• A NRB gift to the children, residue to spouse.

- A gift of the half share of the first spouse to die to adult children.

- A NRB discretionary trust.

- A NRB discretionary trust, the residue to spouse; the trustees can accept an IOU for the NRB legacy or impose a charge.

Chapter 26

Survivorship Clauses

INTRODUCTION

26.1　Why include a survivorship clause in a will? There are four reasons for including a survivorship clause in a will:

- control of the ultimate destination of the assets;
- commorientes;
- avoiding the expense of double administration;
- IHT.

Example

1.　S1 makes a will:

　　To S2, but if S2 predeceases, then to the children.

　　S2's will:

　　To S1, but if S1 predeceases, then to the children.

2.　S1 makes a will:

　　To S2, but if S2 predeceases, to A.

　　S2's will:

　　To S1, but if S1 predeceases, to B.

CONTROL OF THE ULTIMATE DESTINATION OF THE ASSETS

26.2　This is only relevant if the default beneficiaries are different. In example 1, the question of control is irrelevant because the ultimate beneficiaries are the same, and so it does not matter if S1 or S2 dies first.

Where the default beneficiaries are different, however, and there is no survivorship clause, the assets of the first one to die will pass to the survivor, and the assets will then pass to the residuary beneficiaries under the will of the surviving spouse. In example 2, if S1 dies first, and S2 dies one week later, S1's assets will pass to S2, and then to B under S2's will. S1 would probably have preferred them to pass to A.

COMMORIENTES

26.3   The Law of Property Act 1925 provides that where the order of deaths is uncertain, the younger is deemed to have survived the elder.

If there is no survivorship clause, it makes no difference if the residuary beneficiaries are the same as in example 1, but it will if they are different as in example 2. If S1 is older than S2, and both are killed in a common accident where the order of deaths is uncertain, then S1 will be deemed to have died first, and so his assets will pass to S2 as the younger spouse, and then pass to B under S2's will.

AVOIDING THE EXPENSE OF DOUBLE ADMINISTRATION

26.4   If there is no survivorship clause, the assets will be administered twice. If S1 and S2 die within days of each other, the assets of the first spouse to die will pass to the survivor, and will be administered as part of both estates. If there is a survivorship clause, and the second spouse to die dies within the survivorship period, then the expense of double administration is avoided as the assets of the first spouse to die never form part of the estate of the surviving spouse.

INHERITANCE TAX

26.5   If there is no survivorship clause, the nil rate band of the first spouse to die will be lost. It may be possible to retrieve the situation by a deed of variation. If there is a survivorship clause, and the second dies within the survivorship period, then the nil rate band of the first spouse to die is not lost.

However, there is an advantage in not having a survivorship clause if both spouses are killed at the same time, and the order of death is uncertain. This is because s 4(2) of the IHTA 1984 provides that if the order of death is uncertain, the deaths are deemed to have occurred at the same moment.

However, for succession purposes if both S1 and S2 were killed in the same accident, and the order of deaths is uncertain, then the younger is deemed to have survived the elder.

Assume in example 1 that S1 is older than S2. Both are killed in a car accident, and the order of deaths is uncertain.

For IHT purposes, S1 and S2 will be deemed to have died at the same time.

For succession purposes S1's property will pass to S2, and then to the children, and therefore qualify for spouse exemption.

This means that S1's assets will pass to the children free of IHT.

IS A SURVIVORSHIP CLAUSE IN WILLS ALWAYS A GOOD IDEA?

26.6   If one spouse is much poorer than the other spouse, a survivorship clause may not be desirable for the whole estate—leave a nil rate band legacy to the poorer spouse so that he or she can pass it on to the children utilising the nil rate band of the poorer spouse.

Is a survivorship clause necessary if the gift is to beneficiaries other than a spouse? There is probably little point if the gift is small. It is also possible to claim quick succession or successive charges relief if the deaths are within five years of each other.

The question of the use of survivorship clauses in nil rate band discretionary trust wills has been discussed in the previous chapter.

Chapter 27

Second or More Marriages. Cohabitees

SECOND OR MORE MARRIAGES

27.1 If the parties have children from previous relationships, they will often wish to ensure that their assets pass to their respective children. The surest way to achieve their objectives is for the parties to give a life interest trust to the survivor, with remainder to the children. In these circumstances, tax planning is unlikely to be the dominant factor. Note that the survivor could apply under the Inheritance (Provision for Family and Dependants) Act 1975, and might be awarded more than a life interest.

With many couples, the house is their biggest asset, and they may not have much capital beyond the house. In the circumstances, it would seem appropriate that the life interest for the survivor should be limited to the interest of the first to die in the house, and that the survivor should be given the other capital absolutely. It is more than likely that the survivor will need free access to the capital in order to maintain his or her standard of living, and if it is not given to him then the survivor might succeed in a claim under the 1975 Act. In addition, it may not be economic to administer a life interest in a small amount of capital.

Subject to this consideration, however, most of the schemes discussed elsewhere in this book can be used to save IHT where the parties have been married before.

COHABITEES

Different sex or same sex

27.2 Cohabitees cannot make use of the spouse or civil partner exemption on transfers between themselves.

However, joint owners who are cohabitees will receive a discount of 10–15% on the value of their house. This discount is not available to spouses or civil partners because of the related property rules.

Second or More Marriages. Cohabitees

Cohabitees may wish to ensure that their respective families ultimately inherit their property. If this is the case, then consider a life interest trust or a discretionary trust.

Subject to this consideration, however, most of the schemes discussed elsewhere in this book can be used by cohabitees.

For example, a nil rate band trust coupled with a power to accept an IOU should in theory work for cohabitees, or indeed for siblings who wish to leave their assets to each other.

Example

Assume that the nil rate band is always £300,000.

C1 leaves an estate of £800,000.

Deduct NRB.

IHT at 40% on £500,000 = £200,000.

C2 leaves £600,000 inherited from C1 plus £400,000 personal estate.

Deduct NRB.

IHT at 40% on £700,000 = £280,000. Total IHT £480,000.

If C1 had created a nil rate band discretionary trust and had given trustees power to accept an IOU from C2, residue to C1 on C2's death.

IHT payable on £400,000 personal estate plus £600,000 inherited from C1 less C's NRB less IOU for £300,000 = 40% on £400,000 = £160,000. Total IHT £360,000.

There is a saving of IHT of £120,000.

Chapter 28

Property Abroad

INHERITANCE TAX

28.1 Property is exempt from Inheritance tax (IHT) if the property is situated abroad, and the owner is not domiciled in the United Kingdom. Note that both conditions must be satisfied before the property will be exempt from IHT—it must both be situated outside the United Kingdom, and the taxpayer must be domiciled outside the United Kingdom. If the asset is situated within the United Kingdom, then it will be subject to IHT even if the taxpayer is domiciled outside the United Kingdom. If the taxpayer is domiciled in the United Kingdom, then all the assets of the taxpayer will be subject to IHT, although there may be an offset if the equivalent of IHT has been paid in the country where the property is situated.

Two anti-avoidance rules are relevant. The first is that if a person has been resident in the United Kingdom for 17 of the last 20 years, such person will be deemed to be domiciled in the United Kingdom as far as IHT is concerned, but not necessarily for other purposes.

The second rule is that if a person is domiciled in the United Kingdom, but dies within three years of obtaining another domicile, such person is still deemed to be domiciled in the United Kingdom for IHT purposes, but again not necessarily for other purposes.

DOMICILE

28.2 At birth, everyone acquires a domicile of origin. If the child is legitimate, the domicile of origin will be that of the father.

If the father dies between the date of conception and the date of birth, then the domicile of origin of that child is the domicile of the mother.

If the child is illegitimate, the domicile of origin is that of the mother.

If the child is adopted, then its domicile of origin will be determined as if the child had been born in wedlock to the adopters.

It is easy for a person to change his domicile, and acquire a domicile of choice. In order to acquire a domicile of choice, two requirements have to be satisfied:

1. The person must reside in a particular country.
2. The person must intend to remain in that country.

It is very easy to state the test but it is very difficult to apply to individual cases. Residence in another country for a long period of time will not create a domicile of choice in that country if the person concerned does not intend to stay there permanently. Conversely, a short period of residence in another country may give the person concerned a domicile of choice in that country if he intends to stay there permanently. The acquisition of nationality in another country is some evidence that the person concerned intends to stay in that country permanently, but it is not conclusive. Many people who acquire nationality in another country also retain their original nationality, and so it is neutral as far as deciding where they are domiciled.

In *F and S2 v CIR* [2000] WTLR 505, F was born in Iran, but qualified as an accountant in England, where he met and married H. On qualification, he returned to Iran, and ultimately set up a practice in Iran. For various reasons, he left Iran, and it was difficult for him to return. H lived with F and his children in this country. He became a naturalised British citizen, although the statements on his application form were untrue. He needed a passport so that he could travel—his Iranian passport had expired.

It was held that he was not domiciled in England and Wales as the evidence was that he would have returned to Iran if it had been possible.

In the *Executors of Robert Moore v The Commissioners for HMRC* [2002] WTLR 1471, D was an interior designer who worked in different countries. He was an American citizen, and he submitted income tax returns in the United States, but not the United Kingdom. He was granted limited permission to stay in England in order to work. He also owned a residential property in London.

It was held that he was not domiciled in England and Wales.

In *Surveyor v CIR* [2003] WTLR 111, S had a UK domicile of origin, but he had worked in Hong Kong from 1986, had met his wife in Hong Kong, and had three children, all of whom had been born in Hong Kong.

In 1999 he was forced to relocate to Singapore due to a reorganisation by his employers. He subsequently resigned, and was looking for a job in Hong Kong.

It was held that S had acquired a domicile of choice in Hong Kong.

In *Allen v HMRC* [2005] WTLR 937, D had an English domicile of origin. Following her marriage in 1953, she always lived abroad because of her husband's work. Her husband retired in 1982, and they purchased a house in Spain. The deceased had been diagnosed with Parkinson's disease. Her visits to the United Kingdom were infrequent and short.

The deceased's husband died in 1996, and the deceased went to live with her half sister because of her declining health. At the suggestion of her half sister and her husband she did buy a house next door as they were struggling to look after the deceased.

At all times the deceased maintained the house in Spain, and visited it occasionally. She had no investments in the United Kingdom apart from an account here for everyday expenses.

It was held that she was domiciled in Spain at the date of death.

CAPITAL GAINS TAX

28.3   Capital gains tax (CGT) liability depends on residence or ordinary residence in the United Kingdom. However, a person who is resident here but not domiciled is only liable for CGT on gains or overseas assets remitted here.

WILLS

28.4   Foreign heirship and succession taxation rules may apply. It may be that an English will not be effective to dispose of foreign assets, and so it may be desirable to make a foreign will, and an English will. If this is done, make sure that they do not revoke each other.

HOUSES ABROAD

28.5   *Many clients own houses abroad. They may be holiday homes, or they can also be retirement homes. What is the tax position with regard to these?*

As we have seen, property is exempt from IHT if the property is situated abroad, and the owner is not domiciled in the United Kingdom. Note that both conditions must be satisfied—the property must be situated abroad, and the owner must be domiciled outside the United Kingdom. If the property is situated outside the United Kingdom, but the owner is domiciled here, then it will be subject to IHT.

Property Abroad

CGT liability depends on residence or ordinary residence in the United Kingdom.

So a client domiciled and resident here will be subject to IHT and CGT on foreign property.

If there is a house abroad it may be subject to IHT and the equivalent tax in the country where it is situated, Double taxation relief applies if the deceased owned assets abroad, and was domiciled in the United Kingdom.

If there is no relevant double taxation convention, the foregn IHT can be offset against the English IHT attributable to the property.

Example

O dies leaving an estate of £800,000, which includes foreign assets worth £400,000.

IHT paid on the estate is £200,000.

IHT attributable to foreign assets is $\dfrac{£200,000}{£800,000} \times £400,000 = £100,000$.

If foreign IHT is £110,000, only £100,000 deductible.

WHAT ADVICE CAN BE GIVEN TO THESE CLIENTS WHO ARE GOING TO LIVE ABROAD, AND WISH TO LOSE THEIR UK DOMICILE?

28.6

They must sever all contact with the United Kingdom.

They must sell any houses which they have here.

They must transfer all other assets out of the United Kingdom.

They must keep any holidays in this country to a minimum.

Given the uncertainties about domicile, is there any way of testing the waters? It is possible to make use of s 144 of the Inheritance Tax Act (IHTA) 1984 to test the waters. This applies where a will contains a discretionary trust. If the trustees make an appointment more than three months after the death of the testator, but within two years of death, then it is treated as if the deceased had made the appointment in his or her will. So one way of testing the waters is for the testator to create a discretionary trust. The trustees appoint $NRB + £55,000 + a$ reasonably substantial amount to the surviving spouse, and submit it to HMRC. What is a reasonably substantial amount is unfortunately difficult to define (see "Taxation").

If HMRC accept that the surviving spouse is domiciled here, the trustees can appoint the remainder of the assets in the trust to the surviving spouse, and no IHT will be payable as long as the appointment is made within two years of the death of the testator.

If HMRC do not accept that the surviving spouse is domiciled in the United Kingdom, the trustees may wish to think again.

WILLS

28.7

What advice can we give clients who have houses abroad, which may be subject to UK IHT and the foreign equivalent?

The first piece of advice is that they need to consult a foreign lawyer about the succession laws of the country where the asset is situated.

Secondly, check to see if there is a double taxation convention between this country and the country where the property is situated as this may provide some relief against double taxation.

Subject to that, if the property is subject to English IHT and the equivalent in the country where it is situated, then as far as IHT is concerned, the property should not be given to a surviving spouse domiciled in the United Kingdom. The reason for this is that you can offset the foreign IHT against the English IHT. If no UK IHT is payable because of spouse exemption, the credit for the foreign tax will be lost. It may be better to give the foreign property to a child so that IHT is payable on it, so that the foreign IHT can be offset against it.

If the client has acquired a domicile of choice in another country for IHT purposes, then all their foreign assets will not be subject to IHT in this country. Those foreign assets are what is known as excluded property for IHT purposes. If the non-UK domiciled client gives these foreign assets to a beneficiary domiciled in the United Kingdom, then no IHT will be payable on the death of the non-UK domiciled client. However, it may be payable on the death of the UK domiciled beneficiary.

VARIATIONS

28.8

What can be done if the client has given all assets to the surviving spouse, and this includes foreign assets, so that any credit for foreign IHT will be lost?

What can we do if the deceased was not UK domiciled, but has given foreign assets to a UK domiciled beneficiary?.

Deeds of variation can also be used to retrieve the situation. The foreign assets can be given to a child, and if IHT is payable, then the foreign equivalent can be offset against the IHT attributable to the foreign property.

If the deceased was not domiciled in the UK, and gives foreign assets ("excluded property") to a UK domiciled beneficiary, the UK domiciled beneficiary could preserve its excluded property status by putting the assets into a settlement. However, the tax beneficiary will be deemed to be the settlor as far as the income tax and capital gains tax anti avoidance rules are concerned (See **Chapter 15**).

SUMMARY

Liability for IHT depends on domicile in the United Kingdom, or assets in the United Kingdom.

CGT liability depends on residence in the the United Kingdom.

A person with an English domicile must sever all contact with the United Kingdom in order to obtain a domicile in another country.

Houses situated abroad may be subject to a tax equivalent to IHT in the country where the house is situated.

The foreign tax can be offset against the IHT attributable to the foreign assets.

It may be desirable to give a house situated abroad to non-exempt beneficiaries as otherwise the credit for the foreign IHT is lost.

Chapter 29

The Family Company

BUSINESS PROPERTY RELIEF

29.1   Business property relief (BPR) operates to reduce the value of the property by 100 per cent in the following cases:

(*a*)   property consisting of a business or an interest in a business; or

(*b*)   unquoted shares in a company.

50 per cent relief is available on the following:

(*a*)   shares in or securities of a company which are quoted and which (either by themselves or together with other such shares or securities owned by the transferor) gave the transferor control of the company immediately before the transfer;

(*b*)   any land or building, machinery or plant which, immediately before the transfer, was used wholly or mainly for the purposes of a business carried on by a company of which the transferor then had control or by a partnership of which he was then a partner;

(*c*)   any land or building, machinery or plant which, immediately before the transfer, was used wholly or mainly for the purposes of a business carried on by the transferor and was settled property in which he was then beneficially entitled to an interest in possession.

Shares are quoted if they are quoted on a recognised stock exchange.

Thus, 100 per cent relief is available for the following:

- a business or an interest in a business;
- unquoted shares.

50 per cent relief is available for the following:

- controlling shareholdings in quoted companies;
- assets used in the partnership where the owner is a partner;

- assets used by a company controlled by the owner; and
- assets the subject of a settlement used by the tenant for life for business purposes.

Beware of (b) above—if a person owns property used by a company of which he has control, or a partnership in which he is a partner, they should not sell the shares or retire as a partner before disposing of the other property—or BPR on that property will be lost.

There is a minimum ownership period. The transferor must have owned the shares or business interest for two years immediately preceding the transfer.

It is not every business which will qualify for BPR. Businesses dealing wholly or mainly in securities, stocks or shares, land or buildings or holding investments do not qualify for BPR.

INTER VIVOS GIFTS

29.2 It is possible to claim BPR on failed potentially exempt transfers (PETs). However, the donee must still own the property the subject of the gift, or, if it has been sold, replacement property, at the date of death of the donor.

If the donee dies first, then the donee must own the business property or replacement property at the date of death. The property must also qualify for BPR in the hands of the donee at the relevant time, but the normal two-year ownership requirement does not have to be satisfied.

Example

1. T gives his business to A in 2003. This is a PET. T dies in 2007. A is still running the business—BPR is available.
2. T gives his business to A in 2002. This is a PET. A sells the business in 2004, T dies in 2007. BPR is not available—A, the donee, does not own the property at T's death.

Note that if T survives for seven years after making the PET, there is no problem—it is irrelevant whether or not the donee still has the assets.

BPR will be lost if there is an agreement whereby the shares automatically vest in the other shareholders subject to payment. However, an option to purchase will not usually cause the loss of BPR.

Chapter 30

Farmhouses

AGRICULTURAL PROPERTY RELIEF

30.1   Section 115(2) of the Inheritance Tax Act (IHTA) 1984 defines 'agricultural property' as agricultural land or pasture and includes woodland and any building used in connection with the intensive rearing of livestock or fish if the woodland or building is occupied with agricultural land or pasture and the occupation is ancillary to that of the agricultural land or pasture; and also includes such cottages, farm buildings and farmhouses, together with the land occupied with them, as are of a character appropriate to the property.

Agricultural property thus has a wide definition. However, the relief applies only to the agricultural value. Section 115(3) provides that the agricultural value of any agricultural property shall be taken to be the value which would be the value of the property if the property were subject to a perpetual covenant prohibiting its use otherwise than as agricultural property. If there is a field, agricultural property relief (APR) is only available on the agricultural value of the field. If there is a possibility of planning consent, this will clearly increase the value of the field. However, APR is not available on the full value—it will be limited to the agricultural value.

Section 115(5) provides that the relief applies only to agricultural property in the United Kingdom or the Channel Islands or the Isle of Man.

Section 116 provides that the reduction in value is 100 per cent where the interest of the transferor in the property immediately before the transfer carries the right to vacant possession or the right to obtain it within the next 24 months, or the land was let after 1 September 1995. In other cases the reduction is 50 per cent.

Section 117 provides that APR does not apply to any agricultural property unless—

(*a*)   it was occupied by the transferor for the purposes of agriculture throughout the period of two years ending with the date of the transfer; or (*b*) it was owned by him throughout the period of seven years ending with that date and was throughout that period occupied (by him or another) for the purposes of agriculture.

Thus, the transferor must either occupy the land for two years prior to the date of transfer, or alternatively, if the transferor is not in occupation, the transferor must have owned the land for seven years prior to the date of transfer, and throughout that period it must have been occupied for the purposes of agriculture.

Note that if a farmer is relying on the seven-year qualification period, the transferor does not have to be the person in occupation. APR can still be claimed even though a tenant has been in occupation for the seven years, although in that situation the relief may be limited to 50 per cent unless the transferor is entitled to immediate possession, or will be entitled within the next 24 months, or the land was let after 1 September 1995.

Thus, 100 per cent APR is available in the following circumstances:

(*a*) a farmer who is in occupation and has been in occupation for the previous two years;

(*b*) a landlord who is entitled to possession within the next 24 months or who let the land after 1 September 1995 and who has owned the agricultural property for seven years. The property must have been used for farming by the landlord or someone else.

CAPITAL GAINS TAX

30.2　　Capital gains tax (CGT) will be payable on the sale or other disposal of farmland, but hold-over relief will usually mean that no CGT is payable on any gift.

However, do not forget the free uplift on death to market value for CGT purposes. This of course means that it may be better to dispose of any farmland by will, and avoid any charge to CGT, rather than by an *inter vivos* disposition.

THE FARMHOUSE

30.3　　APR is available in respect of 'such cottages, farm buildings and farmhouses, together with the land occupied with them, as are of a character appropriate to the property'.

The other conditions for claiming APR must be satisfied: the transferor must either occupy the land for two years prior to the date of transfer, or alternatively the transferor must have owned the land for seven years prior to the date of transfer, and throughout that period it must have been occupied for the purposes of agriculture.

Remember that APR applies only to the agricultural value—the value on the assumption that the property is subject to a perpetual covenant prohibiting its use otherwise than as agricultural property. There is some doubt as to exactly what this means when it comes to valuing farmhouses which may be very valuable if sold to anyone whether or not engaged in farming. By how much is the value reduced if the farmhouse is subject to a perpetual covenant that it can only be used for agricultural purposes? Presumably any valuation must take account of the fact that the covenant might be released, and so it is arguable that there should not be a large reduction in value.

An excellent way of reducing Inheritance tax (IHT) is to purchase a farmhouse which qualifies for APR. However, the HMRC look very carefully at claims for APR in respect of farmhouses.

In *Taxation* 15 June 2000, Peter Twiddy of the Capital Taxes Office (now IR Capital Taxes) offered some guidance as to the approach of the HMRC to claims for agricultural relief in respect of farmhouses:

> 'We have regard to the basic principle enunciated by Blackburne J in *Starke v Commissioners of HMRC [1994] STC 298*:
>
>> "... cottages, farm buildings and farmhouses ... will constitute 'agricultural property' if used in connection with agricultural land or pasture provided that they are of a character appropriate to such agricultural land or pasture (that is, are proportionate in size and nature to the requirements of the farming activities conducted on the agricultural land in question) ..."

The CTO asks the District Valuer to consider the appropriate test through the eyes of the rural equivalent of the reasonable man on the Clapham omnibus, and the following criteria may help:

Primary character—Is the unit primarily a dwelling with some land, or is it an agricultural unit incorporating such a dwelling as is appropriate? This criterion might be considered an instinctive test, which seeks to gain a comprehensive impression of the nature of the property.

Local practice—Is it normal for land of this quality, use and area to have with it a dwelling of this type and size? The comparison should be with local functioning agricultural holdings rather than with primarily residential holdings. The underlying purpose is to establish the pattern of the type, size and quality of holdings that function primarily as agricultural properties in the area.

Financial support—Is the size and character of the dwelling com-
mensurate with the scale of agricultural operations appropriate for
the land? We are not considering a strict economic viability test of
the holding, but adding information in context.

Having applied those criteria and such other information as is
available, e.g. a large reduction in the area farmed from the
house, we should then stand back and take a balanced view in
the round—difficult to describe, but you know one when you see
one.'

There have been several cases reported recently where the question of
entitlement to APR in respect of farmhouses has been litigated.

In *Dixon v IRC* [2002] WTLR 175, the deceased was co-owner of a cottage,
garden, garage, outhouses and damson orchard. The orchard was used at
various times for grazing animals. The fruit was sold, but the proceeds were
less than £50, and were not declared for income tax purposes.

On the death of the deceased, it was argued that the property qualified for
100 per cent APR.

It was held that whilst growing fruit and grazing were clearly agricultural
activities, it was a matter of fact and degree as to whether the land here
was used for agriculture; here the property was used as a residence and
garden.

It was also held that the house was not used for the purposes of agriculture.

In *Executors of Higginson v IRC* [2002] WTLR 1413, D lived in a large
lodge surrounded by 134 acres, including 63 acres of agricultural land. He
farmed it until about 1985, but thereafter it was let. On his death, the
farm was sold for £1,150,000, and, of that figure, a small proportion was
attributable to the farmland.

It was held that APR could not be claimed in respect of the farmhouse as
the farmhouse was not 'of a character appropriate to the property'.

In *Lloyds TSB as personal representative of Antrobus, Re v IRC* [2002]
WTLR 1435, A lived in a house dating back to the Tudor period. It had six
bedrooms. It was surrounded by 126 acres of freehold land, and 6.54 acres
of let land. A farmed the land, but the business was not commercially
successful.

It was held that the farmhouse qualified for APR. It was appropriate for
the activities carried out on the farm.

In *Rosser v IRC* [2003] WTLR 1057, D and her husband had owned a
41 acre holding in Wales. They gave 39 acres to their daughter, but retained
2 acres, a barn and a farmhouse. They continued to live in the farmhouse,

and eventually their daughter and her husband assumed responsibility for the farm.

D's husband died first, and a few weeks later D died.

It was argued that both the farmhouse and the barn qualified for APR, but the HMRC determined that they did not.

On appeal, it was held that the farmhouse did not qualify for APR, but that the barn did.

The reasons for the decision were that (i) the first reference to 'agricultural land' within s 115(2) did not include the buildings on it; (ii) the property only comprised two acres; and (iii) the house had become a retirement home and was not a farmhouse within s 115(2), and was not of a character appropriate to two acres.

It is clear that farming clients who wish to retire should not make a gift to their children of the farmland and retain the farmhouse. If they do, they may incur a liability for CGT on the gift, and APR may not be available on the death of the parents in respect of the farmhouse. As far as tax is concerned, it is far better to make the gifts by will as there is no CGT liability on death, and APR will still be available. It is, of course, possible that there will be changes to the law which would mean that this advice will have to be reconsidered.

In *Arnander & Ors Executors of McKenna Deceased v Revenue & Customs* [2006] UKSPC SPC00565 (23 October 2006) DM and his wife CM purchased a farm in 1945, but they did not live in Rosteague House until 1978. DM maintained a flat in London as the couple had many interests.

In 1984 they began to farm the land attached to Rosteague House by employing contractors. DM employed an agent, and discussed with him farming issues. He also kept detailed accounts. DM and CM walked the farm frequently.

The acreage of the farm land surrounding Rosteague House was about 110 acres. The accommodation in Rosteague House was described in one of the sales particulars as: 'long hall, dining room, library, study, drawing room, flower room, main foyer and stairs, cloakroom, rear hall, kitchen, staff sitting room, back kitchen, seven bedrooms, three bathrooms, sewing room, laundry room, staff flat, detached lodge, cottage, music room, garage, gardens, range of outbuildings'.

On the death of DM and CM, Rosteague House was not sold as a farmhouse.

HMRC refused the claim to APR on Rosteague House. On appeal, the special commissioner considered the following issues:

Is it a farmhouse?

Farmhouses

The Special Commissioner said:

> "'From those authorities I derive the following principles. That
> a farmhouse is a dwelling for the farmer from which the farm
> is managed *(Rosser)*; that the farmer of the land is the person
> who farms it on a day-to-day basis rather then the person who
> is in overall control of the agricultural business conducted on the
> land *(Antrobus 2 and Lindsay)*; that the status of the occupier of
> the premises is not the test but the proper criterion is the pur-
> pose of the occupation of the premises *(Whiteford)*; however, if
> the premises are extravagantly large for the purpose for which
> they are being used, or if they have been constructed upon some
> more elaborate and expensive scale, it may be that, notwithstand-
> ing the purpose of occupation, they should be treated as having
> been converted into something much more grand *(Whiteford)*; and
> that the decision as to whether a building is a farmhouse is a
> matter of fact to be decided on the circumstances of each case
> and must be judged in accordance with ordinary ideas of what is
> appropriate in size, content and layout, taken in conjunction with
> the farm buildings and the particular area of farm being farmed
> *(Korner)*.'

It was held that it was not a farmhouse.

If it was a farmhouse, was it of a character appropriate to the property?

The Special Commissioner said:

> 'In my view it is not appropriate to compile an exclusive list of
> relevant factors which are to be considered in deciding whether
> a farmhouse is of a character appropriate to the agricultural land.
> The question is one of fact and degree and any factor could be
> relevant. No one factor is determinative but relevant factors in this
> appeal are: the historical associations; the size, content and layout
> of the house; the farm outbuildings; the area being farmed and
> whether the house is proportionate to the land being farmed; the
> view of the educated rural layman; and the relationship between
> the value of the house and the profitability of the land.'

On the facts, it was held that the farmhouse was not of a character appropriate to the property.

Was it occupied for the purposes of agriculture?

It was held that it was not.

VALUE OF AGRICULTURAL LAND

30.4   Assuming that the farmhouses do qualify, how much is of the value is subject to relief? APR operates by reducing the value transferred. This value is the agricultural value, which is the value on the assumption that the house is subject to a covenant that it can only be used for agricultural purposes. So it is not the full market value.

On the other hand, it could be argued that it is not far short of the full market value as a purchaser would be prepared to pay this in the hope that the covenant would be released.

In *Lloyds TSB Private Banking Plc v Twiddy* [2005] WTLR 1535 the deceased was the owner of a farmhouse. In previous proceedings it had been accepted that the farmhouse qualified for APR (the *Antrobus No 2* case).

The issue to be decided in this case was the value of the farmhouse for the purposes of APR as it is the value subject to a covenant that it can only be used for agricultural purposes in perpetuity.

It was held that normally the agricultural value would be about 30 per cent less than the market value. However, if there was a lifestyle purchaser who would be prepared to accept a lower discount, the discount would be 15 per cent.

In *Pissidarou v Rosser* (2005) Ew Lands Tribunal TMA 4–2005 (a sequel to the Rosser case discussed above) the deceased had left a barn which qualified for 100 per cent APR. The agricultural value was £40000, but the market value was £80000 as there was a possibility of obtaining planning permission. If planning permission had been granted, the market value would have been £120000. The District Valuer assumed that a purchaser would be prepared to pay one half of the difference in value between the agricultural value and the market value assuming planning permission had been granted.

The taxpayers represented themselves.

It may be that the decision would have been different if the taxpayers had had professional valuers involved.

Chapter 31

What Advice should be Given to Clients?

31.1   The views expressed in this chapter are the personal views of the author, and he readily accepts that not everyone will agree with them.

Many of these middle income clients do not have a huge amount of capital beyond the house, which can easily worth in excess of £500,000 in many parts of the country.

The author also takes account of the following:

- there are well-publicised problems with some private pension schemes;
- people are living longer;
- even if the client has a secure index-linked pension, it may not keep pace with wage inflation; and
- there may be a return to high inflation.

Can these clients afford to give away the capital they have apart from the house? In the view of the author, the answer for clients in their fifties or sixties is in the negative. These clients should probably retain this capital in case they need it to provide for themselves.

Clients in their eighties or nineties may be able to make gifts, but they must be certain that they can afford to do so.

What about lifetime schemes utilising the house? The author has never been very keen on these schemes as all involve tying up the house, and it could make it very difficult if the client wants to move, or to release capital from the house in order to maintain their standard of living. There is also the added complication of the income tax charge on preowned assets.

If lifetime giving is not a viable proposition, what is the best way of drafting wills?

At the moment, the best method seems to be the nil rate band discretionary trust coupled with the power to accept an IOU or impose a charge in satisfaction of the nil rate band legacy. As long as there is no problem with the artificial debt anti-avoidance rules, this method enables the surviving spouse to deal freely with the assets of the first spouse, whilst at the same time preserving the nil rate band of the first spouse to die.

However, there is no guarantee that this scheme will not be stopped at some point.

Whilst it is still possible for wills to be varied, there may be merit in spouses giving everything to each other subject to a survivorship clause, and the surviving spouse can then vary the will of the first spouse to die if they so wish.

Index

[all references are to paragraph number]